WORLD ENGLISH 1

SECOND EDITION

Real People • Real Places • Real Language

Martin Milner, Author

Rob Jenkins, Series Editor

Australia • Brazil • Japan • Korea • Mexico • Singapore • Spain • United Kingdom • United States

World English Combo Split 1A
Real People, Real Places, Real Language
Martin Milner, Author
Rob Jenkins, Series Editor

Publisher: Sherrise Roehr
Executive Editor: Sarah Kenney
Senior Development Editor: Margarita Matte
Development Editor: Brenden Layte
Assistant Editor: Alison Bruno
Editorial Assistant: Patricia Giunta
Media Researcher: Leila Hishmeh
Senior Technology Product Manager: Scott Rule
Director of Global Marketing: Ian Martin
Senior Product Marketing Manager:
  Caitlin Thomas
Sr. Director, ELT & World Languages:
  Michael Burggren
Production Manager: Daisy Sosa
Content Project Manager: Andrea Bobotas
Senior Print Buyer: Mary Beth Hennebury
Cover Designer: Aaron Opie
Art Director: Scott Baker
Creative Director: Chris Roy
Cover Image: Slow Images/Getty Images
Compositor: MPS Limited

Cover Image
Church Nossa Senhora do Rosário dos Pretos, Salvador, Brazil

© 2015, 2010 National Geographic Learning, a part of Cengage Learning

ALL RIGHTS RESERVED. No part of this work covered by the copyright herein may be reproduced, transmitted, stored or used in any form or by any means graphic, electronic, or mechanical, including but not limited to photocopying, recording, scanning, digitizing, taping, Web distribution, information networks, or information storage and retrieval systems, except as permitted under Section 107 or 108 of the 1976 United States Copyright Act, without the prior written permission of the publisher.

> For product information and technology assistance, contact us at
> **Cengage Learning Customer & Sales Support, 1-800-354-9706**
> For permission to use material from this text or product,
> submit all requests online at **cengage.com/permissions**
> Further permissions questions can be emailed to
> **permissionrequest@cengage.com**

World English Combo Split 1A ISBN: 978-1-285-84858-7
World English Combo Split 1A + CD-ROM ISBN: 978-1-285-84886-0
World English Combo Split 1A + Online Workbook ISBN: 978-1-305-08949-5

National Geographic Learning
20 Channel Center Street
Boston, MA 02210
USA

Cengage Learning is a leading provider of customized learning solutions with office locations around the globe, including Singapore, the United Kingdom, Australia, Mexico, Brazil, and Japan.

Cengage Learning products are represented in Canada by Nelson Education, Ltd.

Visit National Geographic Learning online at ngl.cengage.com

Visit our corporate website at www.cengage.com

Printed in the United States of America
1 2 3 4 5 6 7 8 9 10   16 15 14

Thank you to the educators who provided invaluable feedback during the development of the second edition of the *World English* series:

AMERICAS

Brazil
Renata Cardoso, Universidade de Brasília, Brasília
Gladys De Sousa, Universidade Federal de Minas Gerais, Belo Horizonte
Marilena Fernandes, Associação Alumni, São Paulo
Mary Ruth Popov, Ingles Express, Ltda., Belo Horizonte
Ana Rosa, Speed, Vila Velha
Danny Sheps, English4u2, Natal
Renata Zainotte, Go Up Idiomas, Rio de Janeiro

Colombia
Eida Caicedo, Universidad de San Buenaventura Cali, Cali
Andres Felipe Echeverri Patiño, Corporación Universitaria Lasallista, Envigado
Luz Libia Rey, Centro Colombo Americano, Bogota

Dominican Republic
Aida Rosales, Instituto Cultural Dominico-Americano, Santo Domingo

Ecuador
Elizabeth Ortiz, COPEI-Copol English Institute, Guayaquil

Mexico
Ramon Aguilar, LEC Languages and Education Consulting, Hermosillo
Claudia García-Moreno Ávila, Universidad Autónoma del Estado de México, Toluca
Ana María Benton, Universidad Anahuac Mexico Norte, Huixquilucan
Martha Del Angel, Tecnológico de Monterrey, Monterrey
Sachenka García B., Universidad Kino, Hermosillo
Cinthia I. Navarrete García, Universidad Autónoma del Estado de México, Toluca
Alonso Gaxiola, Universidad Autonoma de Sinaloa, Guasave
Raquel Hernandez, Tecnológico de Monterrey, Monterrey
Beatriz Cuenca Hernández, Universidad Autónoma del Estado de México, Toluca
Luz Maria Lara Hernández, Universidad Autónoma del Estado de México, Toluca
Esthela Ramírez Hernández, Universidad Autónoma del Estado de México, Toluca
Ma Guadalupe Peña Huerta, Universidad Autónoma del Estado de México, Toluca
Elsa Iruegas, Prepa Tec Campus Cumbres, Monterrey
María del Carmen Turral Maya, Universidad Autónoma del Estado de México, Toluca
Lima Melani Ayala Olvera, Universidad Autónoma del Estado de México, Toluca
Suraya Ordorica Reyes, Universidad Autónoma del Estado de México, Toluca
Leonor Rosales, Tecnológico de Monterrey, Monterrey
Leticia Adelina Ruiz Guerrero, ITESO, Jesuit University, Tlaquepaque

United States
Nancy Alaks, College of DuPage, Glen Ellyn, IL
Annette Barker, College of DuPage, Aurora, IL
Joyce Gatto, College of Lake County, Grayslake, IL
Donna Glade-Tau, Harper College, Palatine, IL
Mary "Katie" Hu, Lone Star College – North Harris, Houston, TX
Christy Naghitorabi, University of South Florida, St. Petersburg, FL

ASIA

Beri Ali, Cleverlearn (American Academy), Ho Chi Minh City
Ronald Anderson, Chonnam National University, Yeosu Campus, Jeollanam
Michael Brown, Canadian Secondary Wenzhou No. 22 School, Wenzhou
Leyi Cao, Macau University of Science and Technology, Macau
Maneerat Chuaychoowong, Mae Fah Luang University, Chiang Rai
Sooah Chung, Hwarang Elementary School, Seoul
Edgar Du, Vanung University, Taoyuan County
David Fairweather, Asahikawa Daigaku, Asahikawa
Andrew Garth, Chonnam National University, Yeosu Campus, Jeollanam
Brian Gaynor, Muroran Institute of Technology, Muroran-shi
Emma Gould, Chonnam National University, Yeosu Campus, Jeollanam
David Grant, Kochi National College of Technology, Nankoku
Michael Halloran, Chonnam National University, Yeosu Campus, Jeollanam
Nina Ainun Hamdan, University Malaysia, Kuala Lumpur
Richard Hatcher, Chonnam National University, Yeosu Campus, Jeollanam
Edward Tze-Lu Ho, Chihlee Institute of Technology, New Taipei City
Soontae Hong, Yonsei University, Seoul
Chaiyathip Katsura, Mae Fah Luang University, Chiang Rai
Byoug-Kyo Lee, Yonsei University, Seoul
Han Li, Aceleader International Language Center, Beijing
Michael McGuire, Kansai Gaidai University, Osaka
Yu Jin Ng, Universiti Tenaga Nasional, Kajang, Selangor
Somaly Pan, Royal University of Phnom Penh, Phnom Penh
HyunSuk Park, Halla University, Wonju
Bunroeun Pich, Build Bright University, Phnom Penh
Renee Sawazaki, Surugadai University, Annaka-shi
Adam Schofield, Cleverlearn (American Academy), Ho Chi Minh City
Pawadee Srisang, Burapha University, Chanthaburi Campus, Ta-Mai District
Douglas Sweetlove, Kinjo Gakuin University, Nagoya
Tari Lee Sykes, National Taiwan University of Science and Technology, Taipei
Monika Szirmai, Hiroshima International University, Hiroshima
Sherry Wen, Yan Ping High School, Taipei
Chris Wilson, Okinawa University, Naha City, Okinawa
Christopher Wood, Meijo University, Nagoya
Evelyn Wu, Minghsin University of Science and Technology, Xinfeng, Hsinchu County
Aroma Xiang, Macau University of Science and Technology, Macau
Zoe Xie, Macau University of Science and Technology, Macau
Juan Xu, Macau University of Science and Technology, Macau
Florence Yap, Chang Gung University, Taoyuan
Sukanda Yatprom, Mae Fah Luang University, Chiang Rai
Echo Yu, Macau University of Science and Technology, Macau

The publisher would like to extend a special thank you to Raúl Billini, English Coordinator, Mi Colegio, Dominican Republic, for his contributions to the series.

WORLD ENGLISH Philosophy Statement by Rob Jenkins

BACKGROUND – LEARNING AND INSTRUCTION

Learning has been described as acquiring knowledge. Obtaining knowledge does not guarantee understanding, however. A math student, for example, could replicate any number of algebraic formulas, but never come to an *understanding* of how they could be used or for what purpose he or she has learned them. If understanding is defined as the ability to use knowledge, then learning could be defined differently and more accurately. The ability of the student to use knowledge instead of merely receiving information therefore becomes the goal and the standard by which learning is assessed.

This revelation has led to classrooms that are no longer teacher-centric or lecture driven. Instead, students are asked to think, ponder, and make decisions based on the information received or, even more productive, students are asked to construct learning or discover information in personal pursuits, or with help from an instructor, with partners, or in groups. The practice they get from such approaches stimulates learning with a purpose. The purpose becomes a tangible goal or objective that provides opportunities for students to transfer skills and experiences to future learning.

In the context of language development, this approach becomes essential to real learning and understanding. Learning a language is a skill that is developed only after significant practice. Students can learn the mechanics of a language but when confronted with real-world situations, they are not capable of communication. Therefore, it might be better to shift the discussion from "Language Learning" to "Communication Building." Communication should not be limited to only the productive skills. Reading and listening serve important avenues for communication as well.

FOUR PRINCIPLES TO DEVELOPING LEARNING ENVIRONMENTS

Mission: The goal or mission of a language course might adequately be stated as the pursuit of providing sufficient information and practice to allow students to communicate accurately and effectively to a reasonable extent given the level, student experiences, and time on task provided. This goal can be reflected in potential student learning outcomes identified by what students will be able to do through performance indicators.

World English provides a clear chart within the table of contents to show the expected outcomes of the course. The books are designed to capture student imagination and allow students ample opportunities to communicate. A study of the table of contents identifies the process of communication building that will go on during the course.

Context: It is important to identify what vehicle will be used to provide instruction. If students are to learn through practice, language cannot be introduced as isolated verb forms, nouns, and modifiers. It must have context. To reach the learners and to provide opportunities to communicate, the context must be interesting and relevant to learners' lives and expectations. In other words, there must be a purpose and students must have a clear understanding of what that purpose is.

World English provides a meaningful context that allows students to connect with the world. Research has demonstrated pictures and illustrations are best suited for creating interest and motivation within learners. National Geographic has a long history of providing magnificent learning environments through pictures, illustrations, true accounts, and video. The pictures, stories, and video capture the learners' imagination and "hook" them to learning in such a way that students have significant reasons to communicate promoting interaction and critical thinking. The context will also present students with a desire to know more, leading to life-long learning.

Objectives (Goals)

With the understanding that a purpose for communicating is essential, identifying precisely what the purpose is in each instance becomes crucial even before specifics of instruction have been defined. This is often called "backward design." Backward design means in the context of classroom lesson planning that first desired outcomes, goals, or objectives are defined and then lessons are mapped out with the end in mind, the end being what students will be able to do after sufficient instruction and practice. Having well-crafted objectives or goals provides the standard by which learners' performance can be assessed or self-assessed.

World English lessons are designed on two-page spreads so students can easily see what is expected and what the context is. The goal that directly relates to the final application activity is identified at the beginning. Students, as well as instructors, can easily evaluate their performance as they attempt the final activity. Students can also readily see what tools they will practice to prepare them for the application activity. The application activity is a task where students can demonstrate their ability to perform what the lesson goal requires. This information provides direction and purpose for the learner. Students, who know what is expected, where they are going, and how they will get there, are more apt to reach success. Each success builds confidence and additional communication skills.

Tools and Skills

Once the lesson objective has been identified and a context established, the lesson developer must choose the tools the learner will need to successfully perform the task or objective. The developer can choose among various areas in communication building including vocabulary, grammar and pronunciation. The developer must also choose skills and strategies including reading, writing, listening, and speaking. The receptive skills of reading and listening are essential components to communication. All of these tools and skills must be placed in a balanced way into a context providing practice that can be transferred to their final application or learner demonstration which ultimately becomes evidence of communication building.

World English units are divided into "lessons" that each consists of a two-page spread. Each spread focuses on different skills and strategies and is labeled by a letter (A-E). The units contain the following lesson sequence:

    A: Vocabulary
    B: Listening and Pronunciation
    C: Language Expansion
    D: Reading/Writing
    E: Video Journal

Additional grammar and vocabulary are introduced as tools throughout to provide practice for the final application activity. Each activity in a page spread has the purpose of developing adequate skills to perform the final application task.

LAST WORD

The philosophy of World English is to provide motivating context to connect students to the world through which they build communication skills. These skills are developed, practiced, and assessed from lesson to lesson through initially identifying the objective and giving learners the tools they need to complete a final application task. The concept of performance is highlighted over merely learning new information and performance comes from communicating about meaningful and useful context. An accumulation of small communication skills leads to true and effective communication outside of the classroom in real-world environments.

Split A		Unit Goals	Grammar	Vocabulary
UNIT 1	**People** Page 2	• Meet people • Ask for and give personal information • Describe different occupations • Describe positive and negative parts of occupations	Review of Present tense: *Be* *Be* + adjective (+ noun) Possessive adjectives	Occupations Countries Nationalities Descriptive adjectives
UNIT 2	**Work, Rest, and Play** Page 14	• Talk about a typical day • Talk about free time • Describe a special celebration or festival • Describe daily life in different communities	Review: Simple present tense Prepositions of time Adverbs of frequency	Daily activities Party words Celebrations and festivals
UNIT 3	**Going Places** Page 26	• Identify possessions • Ask for and give personal travel information • Give travel advice • Share special travel tips with others	Possession Imperatives and *should* for advice	Travel preparations and stages Ordinal numbers Travel documents and money
TEDTALKS		Video Page 38 Eric Whitacre: A Virtual Choir 2,000 Voices Strong		
UNIT 4	**Food** Page 42	• Give a recipe • Order a meal • Talk about diets • Discuss unusual foods	Count and non-count nouns: *some* and *any* *How much* and *How many* with quantifiers: *lots of, a few, a little*	Food Food groups Diets
UNIT 5	**Sports** Page 54	• Describe activities happening now • Compare everyday and present-time activities • Talk about favorite sports • Discuss adventures	Present continuous tense Stative verbs	Doing sports Present-time activities Team sports and individual sports
UNIT 6	**Destinations** Page 66	• Discuss past vacations • Exchange information about vacations • Use *was/were* to describe a personal experience • Describe a discovery from the past	Simple past tense Simple past tense of *to be*	Travel activities Emphatic adjectives
TEDTALKS		Video Page 78 Lewis Pugh: My Mind-Shifting Everest Swim		

Listening	Speaking and Pronunciation	Reading	Writing	Video Journal
Focused listening: Personal introductions	Asking for and giving personal information Contractions of *be*: *–'m, –'re, –'s*	**National Geographic:** "People from Around the World"	Writing about people's occupations and nationalities	**National Geographic:** "The Last of The Woman Divers"
Focused listening: A radio celebrity interview	Talking about daily schedules and free time Verbs that end in *–s*	**TED**TALKS "Eric Whitacre: A Virtual Choir 2,000 Voices Strong"	Writing a descriptive paragraph about daily routines Writing Strategy: Word web	**National Geographic:** "Monkey Business"
General listening: Conversations at travel destinations	Giving personal information for travel forms Rising intonation on lists	**National Geographic:** "Smart Traveler"	Writing travel tips	**National Geographic:** "Beagle Patrol"
General and focused listening: Ordering a meal in a restaurant	Role-play: Purchasing food at a supermarket Reduced forms: *Do you have . . .* and *Would you like . . .*	**National Geographic:** "Bugs as Food"	Writing a recipe	**National Geographic:** "Dangerous Dinner"
General and focused listening: Everyday activities vs. today's activities	Talking about what people are doing now Discussing favorite sports Reduced form: *What are you . . .*	**TED**TALKS "Lewis Pugh: My Mind-Shifting Everest Swim"	Writing an e-mail	**National Geographic:** "Cheese-Rolling Races"
General listening: A vacation	Comparing vacations Describing personal experiences Sounds of *–ed* endings	**National Geographic:** "The Cradle of the Inca Empire"	Writing a travel blog	**National Geographic:** "Machu Picchu"

Split B	Unit Goals	Grammar	Vocabulary
UNIT 7 Communication Page 82	• Talk about personal communication • Exchange contact information • Describe characteristics and qualities • Compare different types of communication	Verbs with direct and indirect objects Irregular past tense Sensory verbs	Communication Electronics The senses
UNIT 8 Moving Forward Page 94	• Talk about plans • Discuss long- and short-term plans • Make weather predictions • Discuss the future	Future tense: *be going to* *Will* for predictions and immediate decisions	Short- and long-term plans Weather conditions Weather-specific clothing
UNIT 9 Types of Clothing Page 106	• Make comparisons • Explain preferences • Talk about clothing materials • Evaluate quality and value	Comparatives Superlatives	Clothing Descriptive adjectives Clothing materials

TEDTALKS Video Page 118 **Diana Reiss: Peter Gabriel, Neil Gershenfeld, Vint Cerf: The Interspecies Internet? An Idea in Progress**

UNIT 10 Lifestyles Page 122	• Give advice on healthy habits • Compare lifestyles • Ask about lifestyles • Evaluate your lifestyle	Modals (*could, ought to, should, must*); *have to* Questions with *how*	Healthy and unhealthy habits Compound adjectives
UNIT 11 Achievements Page 134	• Talk about today's chores • Interview for a job • Talk about personal accomplishments • Discuss humanity's greatest achievements	Present perfect tense Present perfect tense vs. simple past tense	Chores Personal accomplishments
UNIT 12 Consequences Page 146	• Talk about managing your money • Make choices on how to spend your money • Talk about cause and effect • Evaluate money and happiness	Real conditionals (also called the first conditional)	Personal finance Animals Animal habitats

TEDTALKS Video Page 158 **Michael Norton: How to Buy Happiness**

Listening	Speaking and Pronunciation	Reading	Writing	Video Journal
Focused listening: A radio call-in program	Asking for contact information Describing sights, sounds and other sensations The /b/ and /v/, /l/ and /r/ sounds	**TED**TALKS "Diana Reiss, Peter Gabriel, Neil Gershenfeld, Vint Cerf: The Interspecies Internet? An Idea in Progress"	Writing a text message Make a list	**National Geographic:** "Wild Animal Trackers"
General listening: A talk show	Talking about weekend plans Discussing the weather Reduced form of *going to*	**National Geographic:** "Future Energy"	Writing statements about the future	**National Geographic:** "Solar Cooking"
Focused listening: Shoe shopping	Talking about clothes Shopping—at the store and online Rising and falling intonation	**National Geographic:** "Silk—the Queen of Textiles"	Writing about buying clothes	**National Geographic:** "How Your T-Shirt Can Make a Difference"
General listening: Personal lifestyles	Discussing healthy and unhealthy habits Asking and telling about lifestyles *Should, shouldn't*	**National Geographic:** "The Secrets of Long Life"	Writing a paragraph about personal lifestyle	**National Geographic:** "The Science of Stress"
Listening for general understanding and specific details: A job interview	Interviewing for a job Catching up with a friend Reduced form of *have*	**National Geographic:** "Humanity's Greatest Achievements"	Writing about achievements	**National Geographic:** "Spacewalk"
Listening for specific details: At a travel agency Listening for key information	Making decisions about spending money Talking about important environmental issues Intonation, sentence stress	**TED**TALKS "Michael Norton: How to Buy Happiness"	Write about cause and effect Writing Strategy: Make suggestions	**National Geographic:** "The Missing Snows of Kilimanjaro"

UNIT 1 People

A girl in a red dress stands out among Muslim women praying on the eve of Ramadan in East Java, Indonesia.

A GOAL 1: Meet People

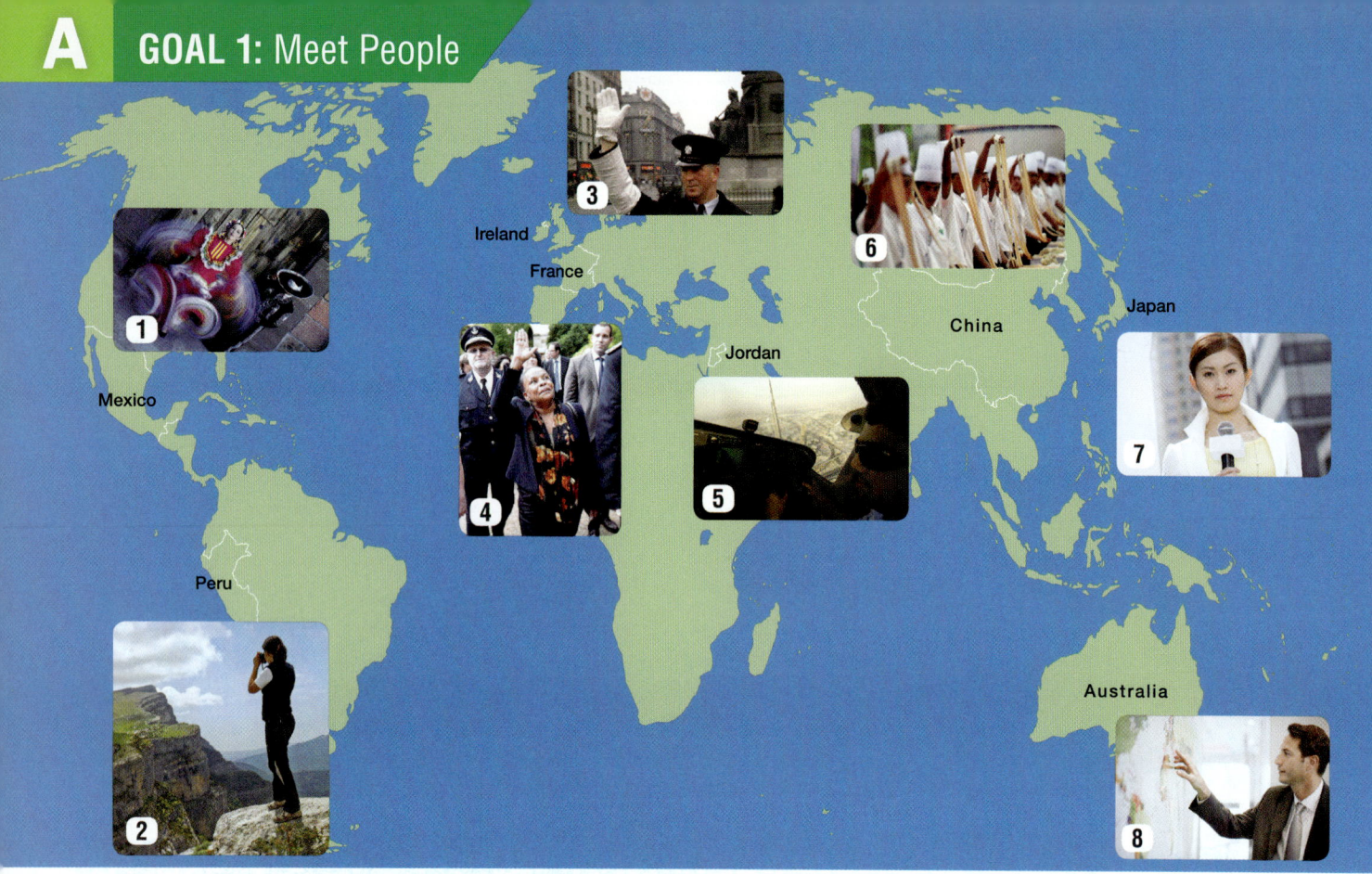

Countries and Nationalities

China — Chinese
Australia — Australian
Jordan — Jordanian
France — French
Mexico — Mexican
Peru — Peruvian
Ireland — Irish
Japan — Japanese

Occupations

~~dancer~~   pilot   chef   journalist   politician
photographer   police officer   travel agent

Vocabulary

A Fill in the blanks. Use words from the boxes.

1. This is Norma. She's ___Mexican___ and she's a ___dancer___.
2. This is Gabriela. She's _____ and she's a _____.
3. This is Frank. He's _____ and he's a _____.
4. This is Marie. She's _____ and she's a _____.
5. This is Yaseen. He's _____ and he's a _____.
6. This is Chuan Li. He's _____ and he's a _____.
7. This is Nanako. She's _____ and she's a _____.
8. This is Nicolas. He's _____ and he's a _____.

B Work with a partner. Talk about the people in the pictures.

> Norma is from Mexico.

> Oh, she's Mexican. What does she do?

> She's a dancer.

Engage!

Rank the occupations from most difficult (1) to least difficult (8).

Real Language

We say *What does she/he do* to ask about a person's occupation or job.

4   Unit 1

Grammar: *Be*

Subject pronoun + *be*		*Be* contractions	
I **am**	Thai.	I'm	Thai.
You/We/They **are**		You're We're They're	
He/She/It **is**		He's She's It's	

Negative statements with *be*

Subject pronoun	Be	Negative	
I	**am**	not	a dancer.
You/We/They	**are**		dancers.
He/She/It	**is**		a dancer.

***Yes/No* questions**

Be	Pronoun		Short answers
Are	you/they	Mexican?	Yes, I **am**. No, I'**m** not. Yes, they **are**. No, he **isn't**.
Is	he/she/it		

A Match the questions and the answers.

1. Are you a doctor? _____
2. Is she Chinese? _____
3. Is Ben Australian? _____
4. Are Mario and Teresa students? _____

a. Yes, he is.
b. No, she isn't. She's Japanese.
c. Yes, they are. They're from Argentina.
d. No, I'm not. I'm a nurse.

B Fill in the blanks with a pronoun and the correct form of the verb *be*.

1. _____ from Japan. I'm from Thailand.
2. _____ from Indonesia? Yes, I am.
3. Where _____ from? They're from China.
4. _____ an engineer. He's a doctor.

Conversation

A 🔊 2 Listen to the conversation. Where is Sean from?

Sean: So, Claudia, where are you from?
Claudia: I'm from <u>Chile</u>.
Sean: So, you're <u>Chilean</u>, eh? Sounds cool. Are you from <u>Santiago</u>?
Claudia: Yes, I am. And you, Sean? Where are you from?
Sean: I'm <u>Canadian</u>.
Claudia: Wow! <u>Canada</u>. I'd love to go to <u>Canada</u>. Which city are you from?
Sean: I'm from <u>Toronto</u>.

B Practice the conversation with a partner. Switch roles and practice it again.

C Change the underlined words and make a new conversation.

D GOAL CHECK ✓ **Meet people**

Choose an occupation, a nationality, and a country for yourself. Walk around the class and introduce yourself to other classmates.

Real Language

To show surprise and interest we can say:

Formal ←→ **Informal**
Really?   *Wow!*   *Cool!*

People 5

B GOAL 2: Ask For and Give Personal Information

Listening

A Look at the pictures. Talk to a partner. Guess the missing information.

B 3 Listen to the TV game show. Fill in the blanks with the correct information.

1. **Name:** Kyoko Hashimoro
   Nationality: _____
   City: Tokyo
   Country: Japan
   Occupation: _____

3. **Name:** Jim Waters
   Nationality: _____
   City: Coldstone
   Country: _____
   Occupation: Farmer

2. **Name:** Luis Gomez
   Nationality: _____
   City: Lima
   Country: _____
   Occupation: _____

4. **Name:** Bianca da Silva
   Nationality: _____
   City: Rio de Janeiro
   Country: _____
   Occupation: Musician

C 3 Listen to the questions in the game show. Write the nationality.

1. **Country:** Jordan   **Nationality:** _____
2. **Country:** Germany   **Nationality:** _____
3. **Country:** Switzerland   **Nationality:** _____
4. **Country:** Jamaica   **Nationality:** _____

Pronunciation: Contractions of *be*

A 4 Listen and repeat.

1. I am   I'm
2. you are   you're
3. he is   he's
4. she is   she's
5. it is   it's

6 Unit 1

B 🔊 5 Listen. Circle the verb or contraction you hear. Then listen again and repeat.

1. (**I am** | I'm) a teacher.
2. (He is | He's) an engineer.
3. (She is | She's) a nurse.
4. (They are | They're) interesting.
5. (You are | You're) welcome.

C Play round-robin.

Student 1: I'm a dentist.

Student 2: I'm a student, and he's a dentist.

Student 3: I'm a teacher, she's a student, and he's a dentist.

Continue the game for as many occupations as possible.

▲ Andrew is a pilot.

Communication

A **Student A** chooses a card from the ones to the right. **Student B** guesses the card by asking *yes/no* questions.

B: Are you 28 years old? **A:** No, I'm not.
B: Are you a doctor? **A:** Yes, I am.
B: Are you Argentinian? **A:** No, I'm not.
B: Is your name Helen? **A:** Yes, it is!

B Choose a famous person. The others in the group ask *yes/no* questions to guess who you are. They can ask 20 questions.

C **GOAL CHECK** ✓ **Ask for and give personal information**

Interview some of your classmates. Ask their name, their age, and the job they do or want to do.

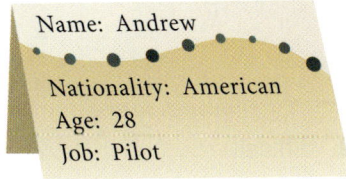

Name: Andrew
Nationality: American
Age: 28
Job: Pilot

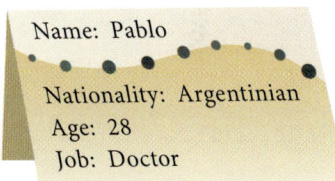

Name: Pablo
Nationality: Argentinian
Age: 28
Job: Doctor

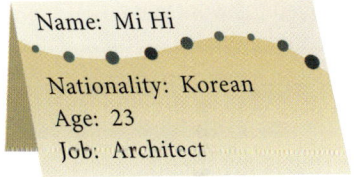

Name: Mi Hi
Nationality: Korean
Age: 23
Job: Architect

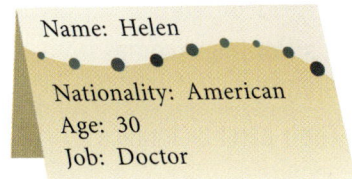

Name: Helen
Nationality: American
Age: 30
Job: Doctor

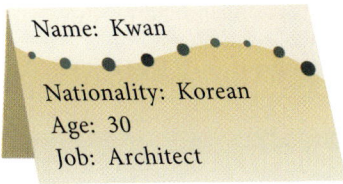

Name: Kwan
Nationality: Korean
Age: 30
Job: Architect

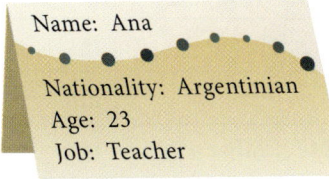

Name: Ana
Nationality: Argentinian
Age: 23
Job: Teacher

People 7

C GOAL 3: Describe Different Occupations

Language Expansion: Descriptive adjectives

 ▲ easy
 ▲ happy
 ▲ unhappy
 ▲ interesting
 ▲ boring

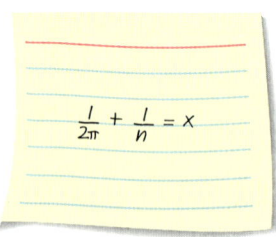 ▲ difficult
 ▲ rich
 ▲ poor
 ▲ safe
 ▲ dangerous

A Write the words in the correct column.

Positive	Negative
happy	unhappy

Word Focus

salary = money earned through the work you do

Possessive Adjectives

This is **my** friend.

Is that **your** brother?

His/Her friend comes from Uruguay.

Their parents are nice people.

*Possessive nouns are formed with an apostrophe (') + -s. Laura**'s** friend is from London.

B Read the sentences. Circle an adjective. Compare your answer to your partner's. Discuss any differences.

1. Dan is a travel agent. His job is (interesting | boring).
2. Ana is a police officer. Her job is (safe | dangerous).
3. Mario's job does not have a good **salary.** He is (happy | unhappy).
4. Ismael is a doctor. He is (rich | poor).
5. Gabriela is a teacher. Her job is (easy | difficult).

Grammar: *Be* + adjective (+ noun)

Subject	Be	Adjective
My friend	is	rich.
His job	is	dangerous.
I	am	not happy.
My brother's job	is	interesting.

Subject	Be	Article	Adjective	Noun
It	is	an	easy	job.
Your friend	is	an	interesting	person.
It	is	a	difficult	life.

8 Unit 1

Victor is an environmentalist. His job is interesting and dangerous.

A Circle the correct word or phrase in parentheses.

1. My father's job is (interesting | an interesting). He is a newspaper photographer. It's not (easy | an easy) job, but he enjoys it.
2. I am a travel agent. The salary isn't very (good | an good). I'm not (rich | an rich).
3. John is an engineer. It's (difficult | a difficult) job, but it's (interesting | an interesting) job.

B Complete the sentences using a possessive adjective.

1. I am a farmer. _____ salary is not very good.
2. Michael is a musician. _____ job is interesting.
3. Susan and Jenny are from Ireland. _____ nationality is Irish.
4. You are a pilot. I think _____ job is dangerous.
5. Michelle is from Germany. _____ nationality is German.

C Unscramble the words to write sentences.

1. job   friend's   is   My   dangerous.   _____
2. is   person.   interesting   Kim's   friend   an   _____
3. your   happy?   brother   Is   _____
4. rich   is   not   a   My   father   man.   _____

Conversation

A 🔊 6 Listen to the conversation. What does Graham do?

Graham: What do you do, Elsa?
Elsa: I'm <u>an engineer</u>.
Graham: <u>An engineer</u>! That's interesting.
Elsa: Yes, but it's difficult work. And you, Graham? What do you do?

Graham: I'm <u>a policeman</u>.
Elsa: <u>A policeman</u>! Is it dangerous?
Graham: No. In fact, sometimes it's boring.

B Practice the conversation with a partner. Switch roles and practice it again. Then change the underlined words and make a new conversation.

C **GOAL CHECK** ✓ **Describe different occupations**

Choose an occupation and say two things to your partner about it. Take turns.

People 9

D GOAL 4: Describe Positive and Negative Parts of Occupations

Reading

A Look at the pictures. What do you think these people do?

B Read the article. Circle **T** for *true* and **F** for *false*.

1. Peter is a pilot. **T F**
2. Peter's salary is good. **T F**
3. Rimii is from India. **T F**
4. She says her work is sometimes interesting. **T F**
5. Tanya is an engineer. **T F**
6. She says school is difficult. **T F**

C Answer the questions.

1. What does Peter do?
   _____
2. Is Peter poor?
   _____
3. What does Rimii do?
   _____
4. Is her salary good?
   _____
5. Where is Tanya from?
   _____
6. Do you think Tanya is happy?
   _____

PEOPLE FROM AROUND THE WORLD

For some people, their job is interesting, but their salary is not good. For other people, their job is boring, but their salary is good. And then for some lucky people, their job is interesting, and their salary is good.

Let's look at some people and their jobs:

Peter Elworthy is from New Zealand. He is not a pilot; he's a farmer! His farm is very big,

so he uses an airplane. He says, "I'm happy. My job is interesting, and also the salary is good. And my dog, Shep, can come with me in the airplane."

Rimii Sen is an actress. She is Indian, and she is from Mumbai. "People think an actress's life is exciting, but it is difficult work, and sometimes it is boring. However, the salary is very good!"

Tanya Rogers is a student from Boulder, Colorado, in the United States. She is studying to be an engineer, but she really wants to be a musician. "School is boring, and I love my music. For some musicians, the salary is good, but for most musicians it is not good."

Engineer or musician? What a decision!

D GOAL 4: Describe Positive and Negative Parts of Occupations

Safi

▲ Angeline

▲ Asef

Communication

A With a partner, make a list of all the jobs you know. Individually, write them in the boxes in the chart below.

	Good salary	Poor salary
Interesting		dancer
Boring		

B Compare your answers with your partner's.

Writing

A Look at the people. Write about each person's job and nationality.

Safi: Afghanistan

Safi is ___Afghani___ and ___he is a farmer._____

Angeline: Brazil

Angeline is _____ and _____

Asef: Jordan

Asef is _____ and _____

B GOAL CHECK ✓ **Describe positive and negative parts of occupations**

With a partner, talk about a friend or family member and his or her occupation. Describe good and bad things.

VIDEO JOURNAL: *The Last of the Woman Divers* **E**

A bay on Jeju Island

Before You Watch

A Fill in the blanks. Use the words in the box.

> tour guide   divers   seafood

In Korea, there is a group of woman _____. They go to the sea every day to catch _____, like octopus and shellfish. Some of the women are not divers. One of them works with tourists. She is a _____.

While You Watch

A ▶ Watch the video. Circle **T** for *true* and **F** for *false*.

1. Diving is difficult and dangerous.   T F
2. The water is cold.   T F
3. The divers can stay underwater for ten minutes.   T F
4. Sunny Hong is a diver.   T F
5. The women sell the seafood.   T F

After You Watch

A Sunny Hong speaks English. She is a tour guide. She is not a diver. She says, "I am lucky." How can speaking English help *you*?

Communication

A What jobs do women do well? What jobs do men do well? Make a list in your notebook.

B Work with a partner. Compare your lists. Are they the same? Do you agree with your partner?

People   13

UNIT 2
Work, Rest, and Play

Parents sleep in the gymnasium of Central China Normal University after accompanying their children to their first day of school.

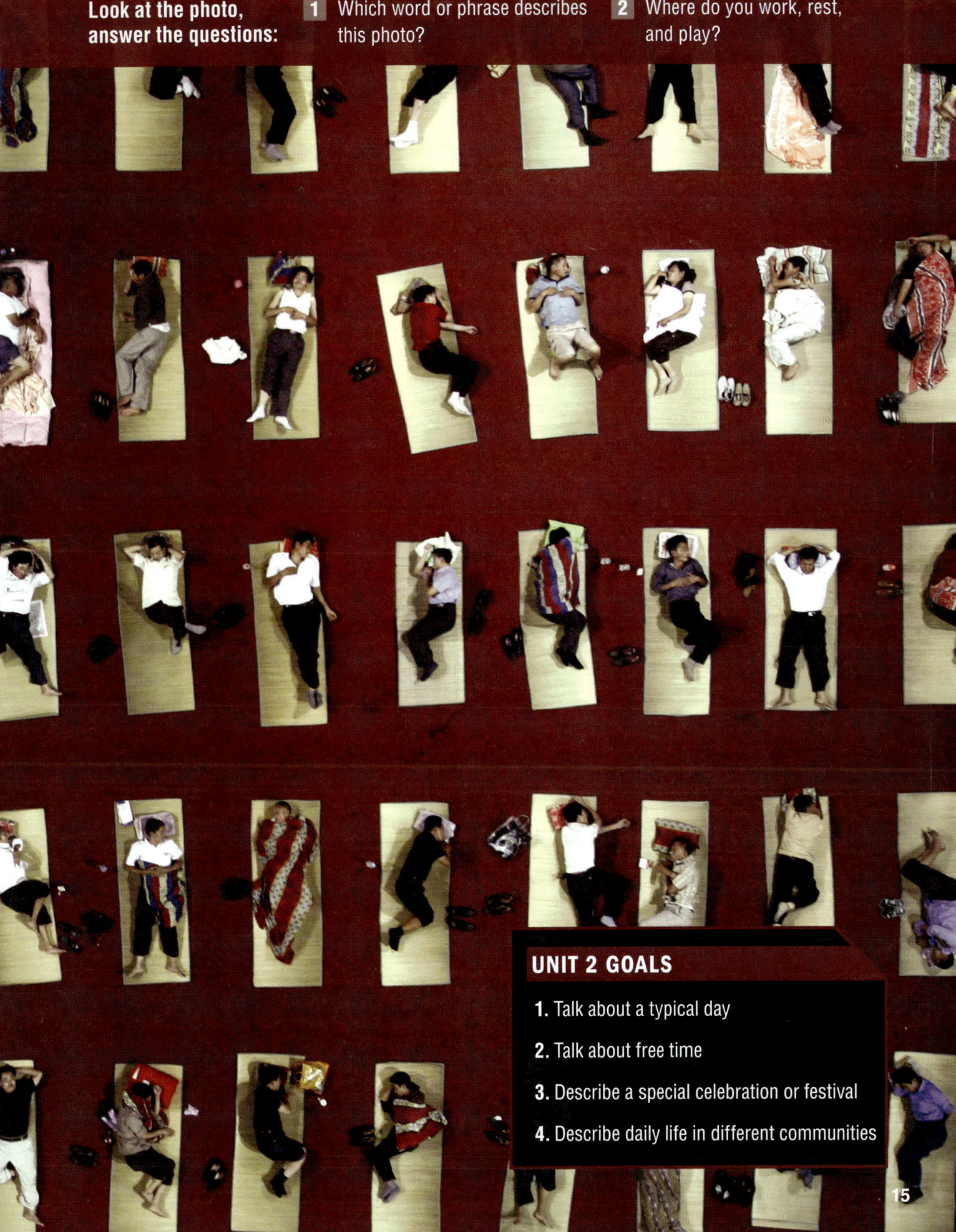

Look at the photo, answer the questions:

1 Which word or phrase describes this photo?

2 Where do you work, rest, and play?

UNIT 2 GOALS

1. Talk about a typical day
2. Talk about free time
3. Describe a special celebration or festival
4. Describe daily life in different communities

A GOAL 1: Talk About a Typical Day

brush your teeth
get up
eat breakfast
go to bed
take a shower
catch the bus
go to the movies
take a nap
watch TV
visit friends
start work
eat out

Vocabulary

A Label the pictures. Use phrases from the box.

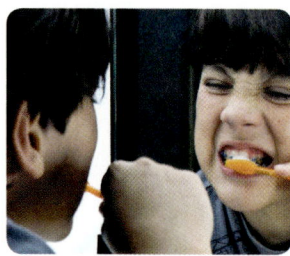  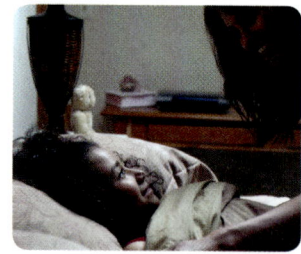

a. _____ b. _____ c. _____

d. _____ e. _____ f. _____

g. _____ h. _____ i. _____

  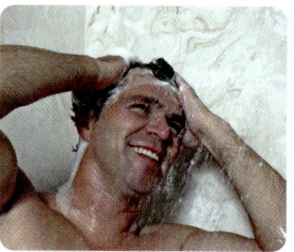

j. _____ k. _____ l. _____

B Circle the activities in exercise **A** that you do every day.

C Make a list of other activities you do every day. Share your list with the class.

D In your notebook, write the activities from **A** and **C** that you do, in the order that you do them.

E Describe your weekday routine to a partner. Use *first*, *next*, *then*, and *finally*.

> **First** I get up, and **then** I take a shower and brush my teeth.

16 Unit 2

Grammar: Simple present tense

Simple present tense	
Statements	**Negative**
I/You **start** work at eight o'clock. Alison **catches** the bus at five thirty. We/They **go** to the movies every Saturday.	I/You **don't start** work at nine o'clock. Alison **doesn't catch** the bus at six thirty. We/They **don't go** to the movies every Friday.
Yes/No questions	**Short answers**
Do you **start** work at eight o'clock? **Does** Alison **catch** the bus at five thirty? **Do** we/they **go** to the movies every Saturday?	Yes, I **do**. No, I **don't**. Yes, she **does**. No, she **doesn't**. Yes, we/they **do**. No, we/they **don't**.

*We use the simple present tense to talk about habits and things that are always true.

A Complete the questions and answers.

1. **Q:** What time do you _____?
   A: I get up _____ seven o'clock.
2. **Q:** _____ you watch TV in the morning?
   A: No, I _____ watch TV in the morning.
3. **Q:** Do they _____ at ten o'clock?
   A: No, they _____ to bed at ten o'clock.

Prepositions of time		
on	**in**	**at**
on Saturday(s) on the 4th of July on Valentine's Day on the weekend	in the morning in the afternoon in the evening	at eight o'clock at night

Conversation

A 🔊 7 Listen to the conversation. Does Mia work on Saturday?

Omar: So, Mia, you're <u>a secretary</u>.
Mia: That's right.
Omar: What time do you start work?
Mia: At <u>nine o'clock</u>.
Omar: Do you work on Saturday?
Mia: <u>Yes, I do, but we finish work at twelve o'clock on Saturdays</u>.
Omar: What do you do in the evenings?
Mia: <u>I watch TV or go to the movies</u>.

B Practice the conversation with a partner. Switch roles and practice it again.

▲ Sara starts work at her job as a meteorologist at seven o'clock.

C Change the underlined words and make a new conversation.

D **GOAL CHECK** ✓ **Talk about a typical day**

Talk with your partner about what you do on Sundays. Mention the times you do each activity.

Work, Rest, and Play

B GOAL 2: Talk About Free Time

Listening

A 🔊 8 Listen to the interview. What is Bob talking about? Circle the correct answer.

a. his daily routine   b. his free time   c. his work

B 🔊 8 Listen again. Circle the correct answer.

1. On Sundays, Bob gets up at _____.
   a. eight o'clock   b. nine o'clock   c. ten o'clock
2. In the morning he _____.
   a. takes a nap   b. visits friends   c. goes to a movie
3. What does he do in the afternoon?
   a. He has lunch.   b. He watches sports on TV.   c. He visits friends.
4. What does he do in the evening?
   a. He watches TV.   b. He goes out for dinner.   c. He visits friends.

Pronunciation: Verbs that end in -s

A 🔊 9 Listen and check (✓) the correct column.

	Ends with /s/	Ends with /z/	Ends with /ɪz/
starts			
comes			
catches			
watches			
gets			
eats			
goes			

18 Unit 2

B 🔊 9 Listen again. Repeat the words.

C ♻ Use the verbs from exercise **A** and write sentences. Have your partner read your sentences and check the pronunciation.

Communication

A Use the cues to write questions.

1. go to the movies / Saturdays *Do you go to the movies on Saturdays?*

2. get up / eight o'clock / the weekend _____

3. watch TV / Sunday mornings _____

4. take a nap / afternoon / weekend _____

5. eat out / weekend _____

B 👥 Interview two classmates. Use the questions in exercise **A**. Write *yes* or *no* in the chart.

Question	Classmate's name _____	Classmate's name _____
1.		
2.		
3.		
4.		
5.		

C ♻ Tell a partner about the interviews.

> Ana goes to the movies on Saturdays, and so does Sebastian.

> Ana goes to the movies on Saturdays, but Sebastian doesn't.

> Ana doesn't go to the movies on Saturdays, but Sebastian does.

> Ana doesn't go to the movies on Saturdays, and neither does Sebastian.

D ♻ **GOAL CHECK** ✓ **Talk about free time**

Talk with a partner about your free time.

> What do you do in your free time?

Word Focus

We use *so do/does* to connect two affirmative sentences.

We use *neither do/does* to connect two negative sentences.

We use *but* when the sentences are different.

C   GOAL 3: Describe a Special Celebration or Festival

People in India enjoy Diwali, the Festival of Lights. They **decorate** streets and houses in many colors.

In the United States, Americans end their Independence Day celebrations with **fireworks**.

In Venice, people wear **costumes** and cover their faces with **masks** to celebrate Carnival.

Language Expansion: Party words

A Read the text and captions. Pay attention to the words in **blue**.

> All around the world, people need to **celebrate**. During the week we work, on weekends we rest, but we also need to have **fun**. **Festivals** are special celebrations. During festivals people dance, sing, wear different clothes, eat special food, and give **presents** to friends and family.

B Complete the sentences with the words in **blue**.

1. We watch the _____ on New Year's Eve.
2. I love parties. You can dance and sing. It's _____ !
3. At Halloween, children wear _____ and _____ to cover their faces.
4. We _____ Christmas on the 24th and 25th of December.
5. I always give my mother _____ on her birthday.
6. I like to _____ the house for holidays.

C Discuss the following questions about your country with a partner.

1. Do you watch fireworks? If so, when?
2. Do you wear costumes? If so, when?
3. Do you give presents? If so, when?

20   Unit 2

Grammar: Adverbs of frequency

0% ── 100%
  never   sometimes   often   always

Word order			
Subject	**Adverb of frequency**	**Verb**	
We	**always**	give	presents at Christmas.
We	**never**	dance	in the streets at Christmas.
Subject	*Be*	**Adverb of frequency**	
Christmas	is	**always**	in December.
Carnival	is	**usually**	in February or March.

*We use adverbs of frequency to say how often we do something.   *Adverbs of frequency come **before** the verb unless the verb is **be**.

A Unscramble the words to make sentences. Write the sentences.

1. always   We   have   a   on   Thanksgiving.   turkey   _____
2. Valentine's Day.   never   I   send   cards   on   _____
3. sometimes   on   visit   our   We   neighbors   New Year's.   _____
4. Nur   his   forgets   wife's   sometimes   birthday.   _____
5. is   in   summer.   It   hot   usually   _____

B Take turns. Tell a partner which sentences in exercise **A** are true for you.

Conversation

A 🔊 10 Listen to the conversation. Does Chuck have a family meal on New Year's Eve?

Diego: What do you do on <u>New Year's Eve</u>?
Chuck: Well, we <u>sometimes go downtown. There are fireworks. It's really pretty. Other people invite friends to their house and they have a party</u>.
Diego: Do you give presents to your friends and family?
Chuck: <u>No, we never give presents on New Year's Eve</u>.
Diego: Do you have a meal with your family?
Chuck: No, we do that on Christmas. On <u>New Year's Eve</u> we <u>just have a party</u>!

> **Real Language**
>
> We say we *party* when we have fun with family or friends.

B Practice the conversation with a partner. Switch roles and practice it again.

C Change the underlined words and make a new conversation.

D GOAL CHECK ✓ Describe a special celebration or festival

Talk with a partner about your favorite celebration or festival.

D GOAL 4: Describe Daily Life in Different Communities

Reading

A Look at the pictures. What kind of music does each show? Discuss with a partner.

B In pairs, talk about your favorite types of music. When and where do you listen to music?

C Read the article. Choose the correct answer.

1. As a child, Eric Whitacre wanted to be _____ .
   a. a teacher c. a composer
   b. in a band

2. When Eric Whitacre _____ for the first time, it surprised him.
   a. wrote music
   b. sang with a choir
   c. met a conductor

3. He became a famous conductor and _____ .
   a. composer c. student
   b. singer

4. _____ makes it possible for people all over the world to join Eric Whitacre's virtual choir.
   a. Pop music c. The Internet
   b. College

5. The people in the choir are united by _____ .
   a. a love of singing c. family
   b. living near each other

WORD BANK
choir group of people that sing together
choral related to a choir
composer person who writes music
conductor person who leads a choir
virtual on computers or on the Internet

Eric Whitacre Composer/Conductor

A VIRTUAL CHOIR 2,000 VOICES STRONG

The following article is about Eric Whitacre. After Unit 3, you'll have the opportunity to watch some of Whitacre's TED Talk and learn more about his idea worth spreading.

Eric Whitacre is a **composer** and **conductor.** He is excited about using **choral** music to join people together from all around the world.

As a child, Eric Whitacre lived in a small town with many farms. He loved music. He didn't know how to read music, but he often played instruments. He always wanted to be part of a rock or pop band. Years later, he went to college. There he met the conductor of the college's **choir.** At first, Eric didn't want to join the choir, but finally he did.

The first time that Eric Whitacre sang with the choir, it was a big surprise. He thought that choral music was beautiful and interesting. He learned how to read music, and then he began to write musical pieces. He became a successful composer and conductor.

Whitacre's choir is very unusual because it's completely **virtual.** The Internet makes this possible. The members of the choir don't know each other. They are different ages, from different countries, and have different professions. But they are united by their love of singing and their desire to be part of a worldwide community that makes beautiful music.

"The most transformative experience I've ever had . . . I felt for the first time in my life that I was part of something bigger than myself."

— Eric Whitacre

A choir blends many voices together to make music.

D GOAL 4: Describe Daily Life in Different Communities

Writing Strategy

A word web can help you brainstorm and organize ideas before you write.

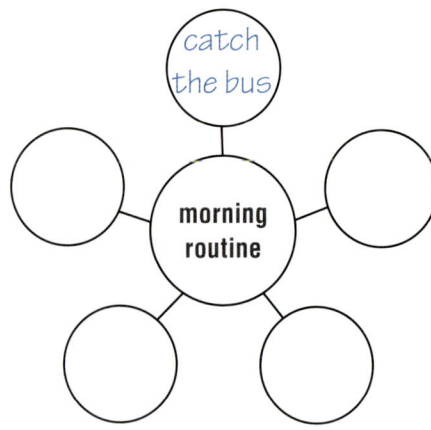

The virtual choir enables people who begin their daily routines at very different times to come together and make music. At 8 a.m. in the United States, Melody is waking up. What time is it for Georgie and Cheryl Ang? What do you think they are doing?

Writing

A Complete the paragraph about a singer's morning routine.

In the morning, I _____ early, around 6:30. Next to my room is the bathroom, where I _____ . Then, I _____ in the kitchen. I never watch TV at breakfast; I often _____ to music.

B Fill in the word web with activities that are related to morning routines.

C Make a word web about your daily routine. Then write a paragraph describing your day. With a partner, talk about how the singer's lifestyle is the same or different than yours.

Communication

A Eric Whitacre always spent a lot of his free time making music. Now he's a famous composer and conductor. With a partner, talk about the following: What do you love to do in your free time? What is your dream job? Are they related?

B **GOAL CHECK** ✓ **Describe daily life in different communities**

Read the paragraph on the left. Pick a singer from the virtual choir. Imagine his or her daily routine. With a partner, write a paragraph describing the day. Talk about how the singer's lifestyle is the same or different than yours.

Georgie from England   **Cheryl Ang from Singapore**   **Melody Myers from the U.S.**

Monkeys in Lopburi

VIDEO JOURNAL: Monkey Business

Before You Watch

A You are going to watch a video about a monkey festival. Circle five words or expressions you think you will hear in the video.

food	take a nap
dance	watch TV
visit friends	water
presents	tourist

While You Watch

A ▶ Watch the video. Circle **T** for *true* or **F** for *false*.

1. The monkey festival is on the last Sunday in November.   T   F
2. The monkeys dance.   T   F
3. The people give the monkeys lots of food.   T   F
4. The monkeys cut the electric and telephone cables.   T   F

B ▶ Watch the video again and answer the questions.

1. In which country is Lopburi?
2. What do the people do for the monkey festival?
3. What is the first goal of the festival?
4. What is the second goal of the festival?

After You Watch

The monkeys of Lopburi are interesting because in other countries, monkeys don't live with people. They are **wild**. But in Lopburi, they live with people. They are **tame**.

A Write the animals from the box in the correct column. Add other animals.

birds cats cows
lions horses elephants

Wild	Tame

Work, Rest, and Play   25

UNIT 3
Going Places

Hot air balloons fill the sky above the Cappadocia region of Turkey.

Look at the photo, answer the questions:

1 Which word best describes the picture?

2 What do you do at this place?

UNIT 3 GOALS

1. Identify possessions
2. Ask for and give personal travel information
3. Give travel advice
4. Share special travel tips with others

A GOAL 1: Identify Possessions

Vocabulary

A In what order do you do these things when you travel? Number the pictures.

▲ take a taxi

▲ buy your ticket

▲ board the airplane

▲ go through security

▲ claim your baggage

▲ go through immigration

▲ go through customs

▲ check in

▲ buy duty-free goods

▲ pack your bags

B Complete the sentences. Use a phrase from exercise **A**.

1. After you _____, you can leave the airport.
2. Do I have to take off my shoes when I _____?
3. At the airport, the first thing you do is _____.
4. Many people _____ like perfume and chocolates at the airport.
5. When you _____, you can only take a small bag.
6. Make sure you don't take the wrong bag when you _____ at the carousel.

C What do you do when you are waiting for a plane? What do you do on the plane? Use a dictionary or ask your teacher for help. Share your ideas with the class.

Grammar: Possession

Possessive adjective	Possessive pronoun	Belong to	
my	mine		me.
your	yours		you.
his	his	It **belongs to**	him.
her	hers	They **belong to**	her.
our	ours		us.
their	theirs		them.

Real Language

To ask about possession, we can say *Whose _____ is this?*

A Complete the conversations. Use a word or phrase for possession.

1. **A:** Excuse me, is this _____ bag?   **B:** No, it's not _____.
2. **A:** Is this Anna's bag?   **B:** No, _____ is green.
3. **A:** _____ ticket is this?   **B:** I think it _____ Shawn.

B Answer the questions using *belong to* and a possessive pronoun.

1. Whose passport is this? (Ali) *It belongs to Ali. It's his.*
2. Whose keys are these? (my keys) _____
3. Whose camera is this? (my sister's) _____
4. Whose bags are these? (John and Lucy's) _____
5. Whose tickets are these? (Logan's and mine) _____

Conversation

A 🔊 11 Listen to the conversation. Who does the bag belong to?

Anna: Whose <u>bag</u> is this?
Bill: It's not mine.
Anna: Maybe it's Jim's. Is this your <u>bag</u>, Jim?
Jim: No, mine is <u>black</u>.
Anna: Well, whose is it?
Bill: Maybe it belongs to this woman. Excuse me, does this <u>bag</u> belong to you?
Woman: Yes, it's mine. Thank you so much.

B Practice the conversation in a group of four students. Switch roles and practice it again.

C Change the underlined words and make a new conversation.

D GOAL CHECK ✓ Identify possessions

Give a personal item, like your pen or watch, to the teacher. The teacher will then give you someone else's personal item. You have to find the owner.

> Do you know whose watch this is?

> Does this watch belong to you?

> Is this your watch?

Going Places

B GOAL 2: Ask For and Give Personal Travel Information

▲ Rome is one of the most popular places to travel to in the world.

Listening

A 🔊 12 Listen to the conversations. Where do the conversations take place?

Conversation 1 _____   a. hotel reception

Conversation 2 _____   b. immigration

Conversation 3 _____   c. check-in counter

B 🔊 12 Listen again. Circle **T** for *true* and **F** for *false*.

Conversation 1
1. The man books a window seat. T F
2. The man has two bags. T F

Conversation 2
1. This is the woman's first visit to the United States. T F
2. The woman is staying in the United States for three weeks. T F

Conversation 3
1. The man is staying at the hotel for one night. T F
2. The man has one bag. T F

one	first	1st
two	second	2nd
three	third	3rd
four	fourth	4th
five	fifth	5th
ten	tenth	10th
twenty	twentieth	20th
thirty-one	thirty-first	31st

Pronunciation: Rising intonation on lists

A 🔊 13 Listen and repeat the sentences.

1. I'm going to London, Paris, Rome, and Madrid.
2. I'll be in Rome on June 21st, 22nd, and 23rd.
3. In Rome, I want to visit the Colosseum, the Vatican, and the Spanish Steps.
4. To get around, I can take the metro, a taxi, or a Vespa.

30 Unit 3

B Practice these sentences with a partner.

1. When we are in Peru, we are going to visit Lima, Cusco, and Machu Picchu.
2. We'll be in Cusco on the 4th, 5th, and 6th of October.
3. To get from Cusco to Machu Picchu, you can take a train, bus, or taxi.
4. The taxi is quick, clean, and expensive.

Communication

A Take turns. Ask a partner questions to fill out the immigration form below with his or her information.

> What is your first name?

> My first name is Wahid.

Department of Immigration **PERMISSION TO ENTER**	
1. First name	8. Principal destination in this country
2. Middle name	
3. Family name	9. Hotel and/or street address
4. Date of birth	
5. Place of birth	10. Entry date
6. Nationality	11. Departure date
7. Country of residence	12. Reason for visit
FORM 12a/PTO (Revised08) [Pursuant to Section 211(d)(3) of the IPA]	

B | GOAL CHECK ✓ **Ask for and give personal travel information**

Work with a new partner. Tell your new partner about your previous partner, using the information on the form in exercise **A**.

> His destination is . . .

▲ Children in the Plaza de Armas, Cusco, Peru

Going Places 31

GOAL 3: Give Travel Advice

▲ travel insurance

▲ international driver's license

▲ visa

▲ credit cards

▲ passport

Language Expansion: Travel documents and money

A Complete the sentences. Use the names of the travel documents.

1. You need a(n) _____ to drive a car in a foreign country.
2. In some countries, you need a(n) _____ to enter.
3. It's a good idea to buy _____. Medical bills are expensive.
4. Your _____ is your photo ID in any foreign country.
5. You can buy a(n) _____ on the Internet. But you need to write down or print the confirmation number.

B Talk to a partner. What is the best form of money to take on your trip? Why?

Give an opinion

> I think credit cards are good.

> The best idea is to take . . .

Give a reason

> People steal . . .

> . . . don't accept . . .

> People lose cash.

▲ airline ticket

▲ cash

C Your father is planning a vacation. He usually uses a travel agent. You think he should do the planning online.

1. Write a list of the things he can get online, for example, hotel reservations and museum tickets.
2. With a partner, role-play persuading your father to buy online.

> You should book a hotel online because it is cheaper.

> No, you should ask a travel agent, so you know the hotel is safe.

Grammar: *Should* for advice

Should				
Subject	*Should*	Adverb of frequency	Verb	Complement
You	**should**	(always)	make	a copy of your passport.
You	**shouldn't**		wear	expensive jewelry.

*We use *should/shouldn't* to give advice.

Questions with *should*			
Should	Subject	Verb	Complement
Should	I	take	a taxi from the airport?

*We use questions with *should* to ask for advice.

A Ask for advice. Read the responses and write the questions.

1. **Q:** Should I take the shuttle bus to the airport?
   A: Yes, you should. The shuttle bus is quick and cheap.

2. **Q:** _____
   A: No, you shouldn't. It is hot at the beach. You don't need a sweater.

3. **Q:** _____
   A: Yes, you should. Credit cards are accepted in a lot of shops.

4. **Q:** _____
   A: No, you shouldn't. It's dangerous to carry cash.

B Ask the questions in exercise **A** and give different advice. Take turns with a partner.

Conversation

A 🔊 14 Listen to the conversation. What does Claudia want from the United States?

Ayumi: Hi, Claudia. You know <u>the USA.</u> Can you give me some advice? I'm going to <u>New York in January</u>.
Claudia: Lucky you! How can I help?
Ayumi: First: Should I buy travel insurance?
Claudia: Yes, you should. Hospitals and doctors are very expensive in <u>the U.S.</u>
Ayumi: OK. That's another $200. What about clothes? What should I take?
Claudia: <u>You should take a warm sweater and some gloves and a scarf</u>.
Ayumi: Hmm, that's another $100.
Claudia: Oh, just one more thing! Don't forget to buy me a nice present, like a new <u>watch</u>.
Ayumi: Oh no! That's another $500! Traveling is expensive!

B Practice the conversation with a partner. Switch roles and practice it again.

C Change the underlined words and make a new conversation.

D **GOAL CHECK** ✓ **Give travel advice**

Discuss travel tips for visitors to your country. Think about the following topics.

- transportation
- how to carry money
- Can you drink the water?

▲ Washington Square Park, New York City

Going Places

D GOAL 4: Share Special Travel Tips with Others

Reading

A Read the article. Then answer the questions.

1. Do you think the author enjoys traveling? _____
   _____

2. Why should you check the expiration date of your passport? _____
   _____

3. Why should you tie a sock to your bag?
   _____
   _____

4. Why should you take a good book when you travel? _____
   _____

B Circle **T** for *true* and **F** for *false*.

1. You need a lot of documents to travel.   T   F
2. You need to take a lot of clothes in your bag. T   F
3. Bags can be hard to identify at the airport.   T   F
4. Flights are never late.   T   F
5. Airplane food is always good.   T   F

Word Focus

expiration date = the date a thing comes to an end or can no longer be used

Real Language

We use the expression *share some pointers* to say *give advice*.

SMART

34   Unit 3

TRAVELER

EXPERT OPINION

In his book Easy Travel, *Mike Connelly* **shares some pointers** on making travel easy:

DOCUMENTS Make sure you have all your documents: passport, visas, tickets, etc. You should always check the **expiration date** of your passport. Many countries won't let you enter with less than six months left on your passport. Don't forget to buy travel insurance. Medical bills can be very expensive, especially in the United States and Europe. Finally, you should make copies of all your important documents and credit cards and keep them in another bag.

PACKING My advice is—always travel light! I hate to carry heavy bags. Just take the minimum. There is an old saying: *Breakfast in Berlin. Dinner in Delhi. Bags in Bangkok!* So, don't pack anything important in your check-in bag; put important things in your carry-on bag. You don't want to arrive home without your house keys. Another tip—don't use expensive suitcases. People don't steal dirty old bags. Finally, here's a good little tip—tie a sock or brightly colored string to your bag. Why? So you can quickly see your bag on the airport carousel.

THE AIRPORT My first piece of advice is that you should always carry a good book. It helps to pass the time as you wait for your delayed flight. Don't forget to take a sweater or a jacket on the plane. It can get cold on a long night flight. And then there is airline food. Take a snack (cookies or fruit) with you. Sometimes the food is late, sometimes it doesn't arrive at all, and it's never very good.

D GOAL 4: Share Special Travel Tips with Others

▲ Riviera Maya, Mexico

Communication

A You have won a vacation for two people and you can choose where to go. Choose one of the following and be ready to say why you chose it.

Resort in Mexico
World Cup in Brazil
Trekking in the Himalayas
Historical tour of Angkor Wat, Cambodia
Adventure tourism in New Zealand

B Read the list below—your teacher will help you. You can only take five of these items. Discuss which items to take with a partner. Give your reasons.

1. sun block
2. binoculars
3. warm clothes
4. first-aid kit
5. international driver's license
6. water sterilization tablets
7. umbrella
8. maps
9. money belt
10. guidebook
11. sunglasses
12. hair dryer
13. penknife
14. smartphone

Do you think we should take . . . ?

I think we should take . . . because . . .

I don't think we should take . . . because . . .

Writing

A Write travel tips for your vacation in your notebook.

B GOAL CHECK ✓ **Share special travel tips with others**

Read your travel tips to a partner. Then share them with the class.

VIDEO JOURNAL: *Beagle Patrol* E

Before You Watch

A Do you have working dogs in your country? How do these dogs help people?

While You Watch

A ▶ Watch the video. Circle the names of things you see.

uniform   apples   suitcase   passport   mango   beef jerky

B ▶ Watch the video again. Circle **T** for *true* and **F** for *false*.

1. Brent and Stockton play before they start work.   T   F
2. Detector dogs look for meat.   T   F
3. Stockton does not find the meat.   T   F
4. Stockton eats the meat he finds.   T   F
5. Stockton is learning slowly.   T   F

After You Watch/Communication

A 🗨 In the video, we saw that dogs can be very useful in airports. Work with a partner to write a list of possible problems with dogs in airports.

B 🗨 With a partner, role-play the following situations.

In **Situation 1,** Student A is a dog handler, and Student B is a passenger. The dog is sniffing in Student B's bag, and Student B does not like dogs.

In **Situation 2,** Student A is a passenger that has fruit in his or her bag. The fruit is a gift. Student B is the dog handler and has to take the fruit.

Word Focus

disease   to bother   illegal

Rats are dirty. Sometimes they carry **disease.**

Hey, kids! Please be quiet. I'm trying to work. You're **bothering** me.

You can't park your car there. It's not allowed. It's **illegal.**

Going Places

TEDTALKS

Eric Whitacre Composer/Conductor
A VIRTUAL CHOIR 2,000 VOICES STRONG

Before You Watch

A Write the correct word under each picture.

| singer | conductor | choir | piano |

1. _____

2. _____

3. _____

4. _____

B Work with a partner. Try to think of one example each for items 1–4 in exercise **A**. Share your answers with the class.

C Complete the sentences using the words from the box.

> **community** group of similar people
> **connection** relationship
> **post** put information up
> **record** store music so it can be listened to later
> **virtual** on a computer

1. The sisters had a very strong _____.
2. Please _____ your music for him.
3. People who live in a neighborhood are part of the _____.
4. The video game had a _____ world that players could play in.
5. I will _____ this information on the Web site for my classmates.

> Eric Whitacre's idea worth spreading is that technology and music can connect us in wonderful, unexpected ways. Watch Whitacre's full TED Talk on TED.com.

D You are going to watch a TED Talk about a virtual choir. What do you think you will see in the video? What things do you think a person should do if they are going to start an online community? Discuss them with a partner.

> You should have a computer.

While You Watch

A Look at the pictures and quotes on the next page. Then watch the TED Talk. As you watch, put the pictures in order. Write the number in the box under the picture.

B Watch the TED Talk again. Complete the sentences using the words from the box.

| connect | singers | Malta |
| Sleep | Britlin | Jordan |

1. A girl named _____ posted a video for Eric Whitacre. Her video gave Eric the idea for the first virtual choir.
2. Eric created a virtual choir to _____ people around the world.
3. The second virtual choir had 2,051 _____.
4. The second virtual choir had singers from many countries, such as _____ and _____.
5. Eric Whitacre chose a piece called _____ for the second virtual choir.

38

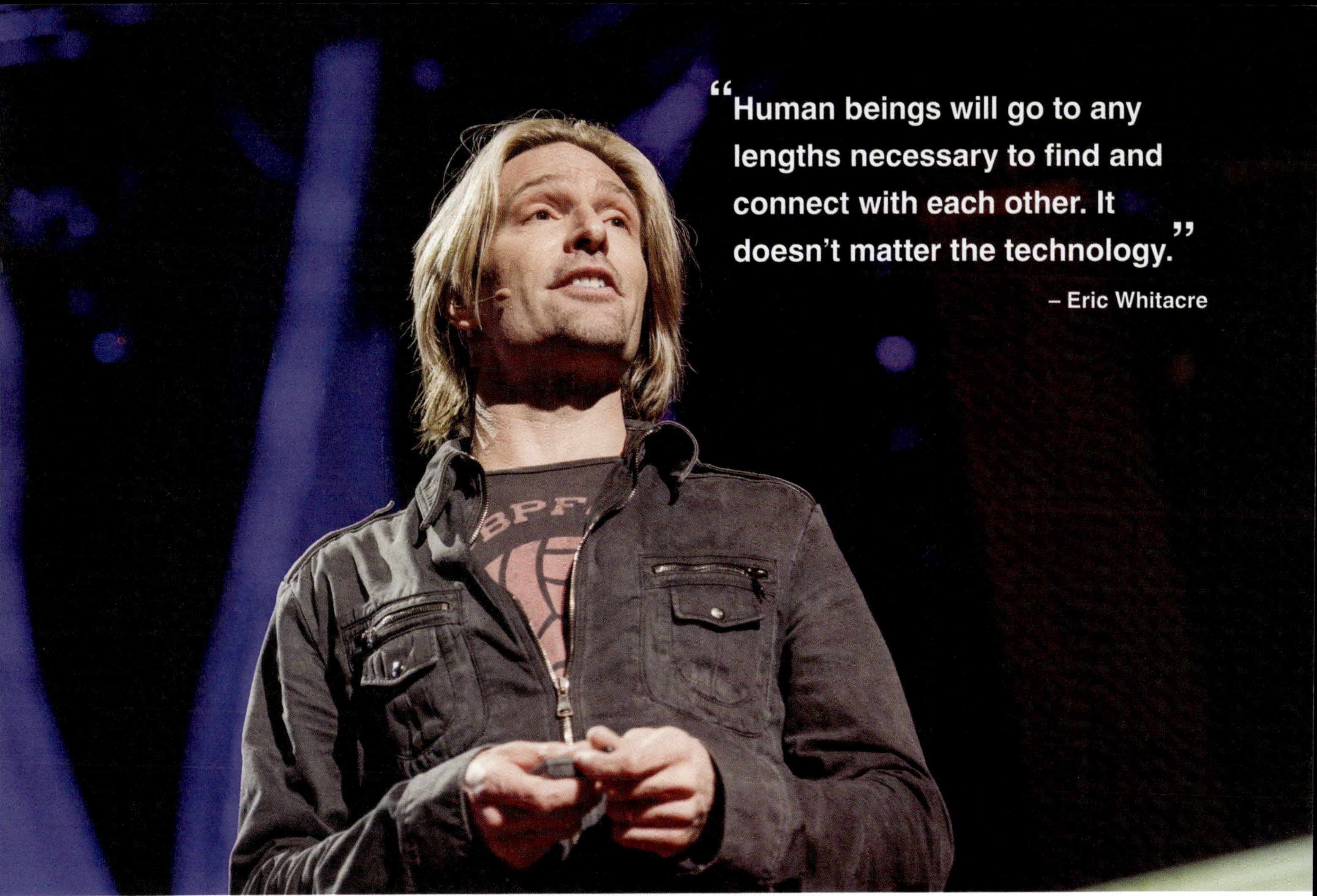

> "Human beings will go to any lengths necessary to find and connect with each other. It doesn't matter the technology."
>
> – Eric Whitacre

☐ "I had this idea: if I could get 50 people to all do this same thing, sing their parts—soprano, alto, tenor, and bass—wherever they were in the world, post their videos to YouTube, we could cut it all together and create a virtual choir."

☐ "I just couldn't believe the poetry of all of it—these souls all on their own desert island, sending electronic messages in bottles to each other."

☐ "For Virtual Choir 2.0 . . . our final tally was 2,051 videos from 58 different countries. From Malta, Madagascar, Thailand, Vietnam, Jordan, Egypt, Israel, as far north as Alaska, and as far south as New Zealand."

☐ "I posted a conductor track of myself conducting. And it's in complete silence when I filmed it, because I was only hearing the music in my head, imagining the choir that would one day come to be."

Eric Whitacre Composer/Conductor
A VIRTUAL CHOIR 2,000 VOICES STRONG

Virtual Choir 2.0

After You Watch

A Read the sentences. Correct the false information.

1. A choir has to use the Internet. _____virtual choir_____

2. In Eric Whitacre's virtual choir, all the singers record their videos at the same time. _____

3. In their testimonials, the singers said that being in the virtual choir did not make them feel connected to other people around the world.
_____

4. All of the members of the choir are now good friends, even though they live in different countries and do not meet in person.
_____

B Most conductors work with singers in person, but Eric Whitacre conducts a choir online. With a group, take turns naming occupations. For each one, discuss whether it is possible for people in the occupation to work in a virtual way.

Teacher
- Teachers usually work in person.
- It is also possible for them to work in a virtual way. Teachers can teach online.

C Someone you know wants to be part of Eric Whitacre's next virtual choir. What advice would you give? With a partner, brainstorm a list of verbs (*be, learn, post*, etc.). Use *should/shouldn't* and the verbs to write five pieces of advice in your notebook.

Rural Alaska

D One woman in the virtual choir lives in rural Alaska, 400 miles from the nearest town. What do you think her life is like? Why is the choir important to her? How do music and technology connect her with people around the world? Discuss with a partner.

E Do you like to do the following things online, in person, or both? Add your own idea. Then answer by placing a check (✓) in the appropriate box. Then interview your classmates about what they prefer. Write each classmate's initials in the appropriate box. Share with the class.

	Virtual world	In person	Both
1. play games			
2. take classes			
3. talk to family			
4. shop			
5. explore the world			
6. _____			

F Pick one of the activities in exercise **E**. Write a short paragraph about why you think it is better to do that activity online or in person. Use some of the words provided.

| to live nearby/far away | to connect | to spend time together/alone |
| to feel lonely/alone | to meet | |

Challenge! What other virtual choirs has Eric Whitacre conducted? Visit TED.com to find out. Then share what you learned with a group. Be sure to include the name of the musical piece, the number of singers, the number of countries, and a short description of the piece. Use at least two descriptive adjectives.

Unit 4 Food

A colorful blend of spices is displayed in a variety of measuring spoons. People around the world use spices to flavor and preserve food.

Look at the photo, answer the questions:

1 Can you name any of the spices in the picture?

2 What is your favorite food?

UNIT 4 GOALS

1. Give a recipe
2. Order a meal
3. Talk about diets
4. Discuss unusual foods

A GOAL 1: Give a Recipe

drinks   dairy products
vegetables   fruit
protein   meat

Vocabulary

A Talk to a partner. Choose a word or phrase from the box to describe each group of foods.

Juice and water are drinks.

B With your partner, think of some other foods you know and write them in the correct group. Then share them with the class.

Grammar: *Some* and *any* with count and non-count nouns

Count and non-count nouns	
Singular	**Plural**
This is a lemon.	Those are lemons.
This is milk.	~~Those are milks.~~

*For nouns you can count, we add *-s* or *-es* to form the plural.
*Nouns you cannot count don't have a plural form.

Some and *any*	Count nouns		Non-count nouns
	Singular	**Plural**	
Statement	We need an apple.	There are **some** oranges on the table.	There is **some** cheese on the table.
Negative	We don't have a lemon.	There aren't **any** bananas at the store.	We don't have **any** milk.
Question	Do we have a red pepper?	Are there **any** eggs?	Do you have **any** butter?

*You can also use *some* for questions with *could*.
 Could I have **some** milk?

44   Unit 4

A In your notebook, write the food words from the picture in two columns: *Count nouns* and *Non-count nouns*.

B Add other food words to the chart. Use a dictionary if necessary. Share your words with your group.

C Complete the sentences with *some* or *any*.

1. Do we have _____ tomatoes?
2. Pass me _____ apples, please.
3. There isn't _____ milk in the fridge.
4. I think there is _____ cheese on the table.
5. There aren't _____ eggs.
6. Could I have _____ water, please?

Conversation

A 🔊 15 Listen to the conversation. What do you need to make a Spanish omelet?

Lee: Let's make a Spanish omelet.
Diana: Great. What do we need?
Lee: OK. It says here you need some olive oil. Do we have any olive oil?
Diana: No, we don't, but it doesn't matter; we have some corn oil. That will do.
Lee: Next, we need some potatoes, a large onion, and a red pepper.
Diana: We don't have a red pepper.
Lee: Never mind. We can use a green pepper.
Diana: OK. And then we need some eggs. Four eggs.
Lee: OK! Let's begin!

Real Language

We can use *never mind* or *it doesn't matter* to show something is not important.

Word Focus

Names of fractions:
$\frac{1}{2}$ = one-half
$\frac{1}{3}$ = one-third
$\frac{1}{4}$ = one-fourth or one-quarter

B Practice the conversation with a partner. Switch roles and practice it again.

C Choose a new recipe and repeat the conversation.

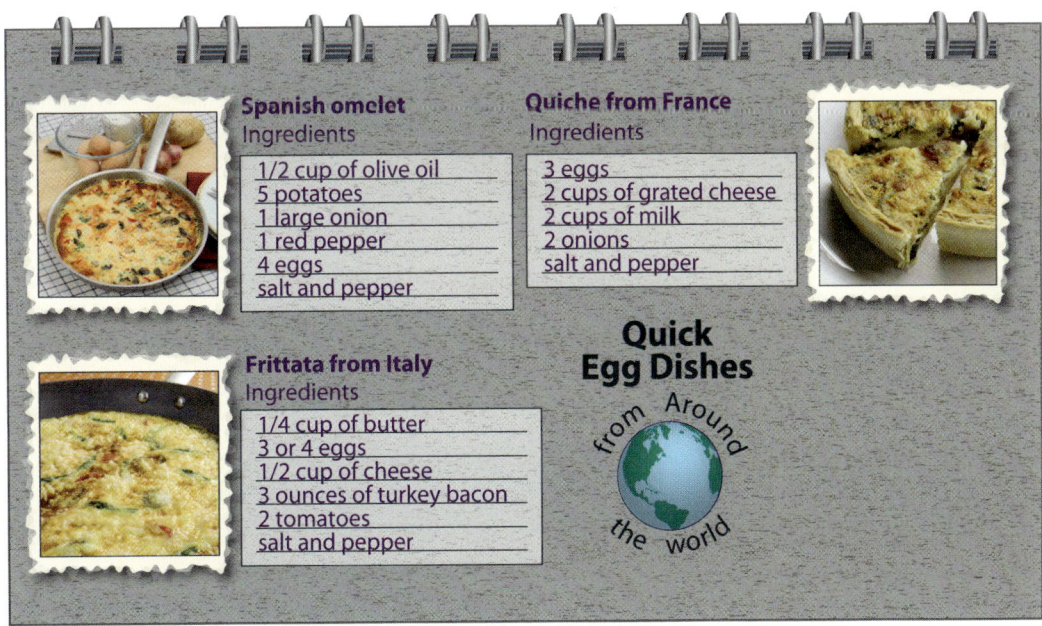

Spanish omelet
Ingredients
1/2 cup of olive oil
5 potatoes
1 large onion
1 red pepper
4 eggs
salt and pepper

Quiche from France
Ingredients
3 eggs
2 cups of grated cheese
2 cups of milk
2 onions
salt and pepper

Frittata from Italy
Ingredients
1/4 cup of butter
3 or 4 eggs
1/2 cup of cheese
3 ounces of turkey bacon
2 tomatoes
salt and pepper

Quick Egg Dishes from Around the world

D **GOAL CHECK** ✓ **Give a recipe**

Tell a partner the name of a dish you like. Explain the recipe by describing the ingredients you need to prepare it.

B GOAL 2: Order a Meal

▲ A busy restaurant in Guilin, China

Listening

A 🔊 16 Listen to the **waiter** taking an order from **customers**. How many customers are there?

B 🔊 16 Listen again and write the food and drink that each person ordered.

	Drink	Food
Man		
Woman		

Menu

Appetizers

Chicken 'n Cheese
Deep-fried chicken served with fresh tomatoes and sliced Cheddar cheese

Vegetable Soup
Made from fresh vegetables

Main Dishes

Seashore Shrimp
Grilled shrimp served with peppers and boiled rice

Butter-Baked Chicken
Roasted half-chicken in a lemon sauce served with carrots and potatoes

Filet Mignon
8 oz. grilled tenderloin steak, served with iceberg lettuce and your favorite salad dressing

Drinks
Mineral water, iced tea, coffee

Word Focus

waiter = A *waiter* is a person who works in a restaurant and serves food and drinks.

customer = A *customer* is a person who buys goods or services.

C 🔊 16 Listen again. Who asked these questions?

1. Are you ready to order? _waiter_
2. Do you have any mineral water? _____
3. What would you recommend? _____
4. Does the filet mignon come with salad? _____
5. Anything else? _____

Pronunciation: Reduced forms *Do you have . . .* and *Would you like . . .*

A 🔊 17 Listen to the full form and the reduced form.

B 🔊 18 Listen and check (✓) the correct column. Then listen again and repeat.

	Full form	Reduced form
1. Do you have a pen?		
2. Would you like some more bread?		
3. Do you have any paper?		
4. Would you like some coffee?		
5. Do you have any change?		

Communication

A 🔄 With a partner, role-play the following situation.

Student A You work in a supermarket. Serve the customer.

Student B You want to make one of the egg dishes on page 45. Ask for the food you need from the sales assistant.

B 🔄 **GOAL CHECK** ✓ **Order a meal**

Work with a partner. Choose roles and role-play. Switch roles and role-play again.

Student A You are a customer in a restaurant. Order a meal from the menu on page 46.

Student B You are the waiter. Take the customer's order.

Food 47

GOAL 3: Talk About Diets

▲ broccoli

▲ cauliflower

▲ beans

▲ whole-wheat bagel

▲ breakfast cereal

▲ nuts

Language Expansion: Diets

Many people eat a special diet. Sometimes, people go on a diet to lose weight and sometimes so that they will feel healthier. Here are two diets: a high-fiber diet and a high-protein diet. The first has a lot of food that contains fiber, for example, whole wheat, brown rice, and maize. The second has a lot of food that contains protein, like meat, fish, and cheese.

	High-fiber diet	High-protein diet
Breakfast	1 bowl of high-fiber breakfast cereal or 2 slices of whole-grain bread or 1 whole-grain bagel fruit	4 slices of turkey bacon or 2 sausages 3 eggs a glass of milk
Snack	popcorn or dried fruit	1 hamburger (without the bread) or 2 beef hot dogs (without the bread)
Lunch or Dinner	vegetables dried pea, bean, or lentil soup berries nuts	1 large steak or chicken cheese

A Write the names of the foods on the page in the correct column.

High-fiber diet	High-protein diet

▲ hamburger

▲ tuna salad

B Add the names of other high-fiber and high-protein foods you know to the chart.

Grammar: *How much* and *How many* with quantifiers: *lots of, a few, a little*

Information question	Quantifiers	
	++++	+
Count — How many oranges do you need?	I need **lots of** oranges.	I need **a few** oranges.
Non-count — How much milk do we have?	We have **lots of** milk.	We have **a little** milk.

*We use *lots of* and *a few* to answers questions about quantity.
*We use *a little* to answer questions about small quantities we cannot count.

A Complete the sentences using *a little* or *a few*.

1. There is only _____ tuna salad in the fridge.
2. We only need _____ apples.
3. Please bring _____ bananas.
4. I only take _____ sugar in my coffee.
5. There are just _____ peppers left.

B Fill in the blanks with *How much, How many, lots of, a few,* or *a little*.

1. Q: _How many_ potatoes would you like?   A: Just _a few_, thanks.
2. Q: _____ steak do we need?   A: There are eight of us, so we need _____ steak.
3. Q: _____ broccoli would you like?   A: I'm not very hungry. Just _____.
4. Q: _____ apples do we need?   A: About 20. We eat _____ apples.

C With a partner, use the words in exercise **A** on page 48 to ask and answer questions.

Conversation

A 🔊 19 Listen to the conversation. Can Pat eat popcorn?

Kim: You're looking good.
Pat: Thanks, Kim. I'm on a special diet. It's a high-fiber diet.
Kim: High fiber? You mean lots of bread and fruit?
Pat: That's right.
Kim: How much bread can you eat for breakfast?
Pat: I can eat two slices of whole-grain bread for breakfast or one bowl of high-fiber cereal.
Kim: And what about snacks?
Pat: No problem. I can eat lots of popcorn and dried fruit.
Kim: Mmm, sounds like a delicious diet. Maybe I'll join you.

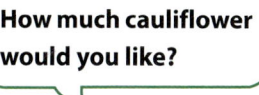

How much cauliflower would you like?

Just a little.

B Practice the conversation with a partner. Switch roles and practice it again.

C Make a new conversation for the high-protein diet.

D GOAL CHECK ✓ **Talk about diets**

With a partner, have a conversation about your own diet or another diet you know.

D GOAL 4: Discuss Unusual Foods

Reading

A Look at the photos. Do people eat insects in your country?

B Read the article. Answer the questions.

1. What insects are on the menu in the restaurant? _____
2. In Thailand, are insects luxury food? _____
3. How many bits of insects are allowed in peanut butter? _____
4. What does the author order? _____
5. Do you like to eat insects? Give your reasons. _____

▲ Crickets, grasshoppers, and other insects-on-a-stick are for sale at a Donghaumen Night Market near Wangfujing Dongcheng, Beijing, China.

Word Focus

luxury = A *luxury* is something we do not really need.

unintentionally = When something happens *unintentionally*, we don't mean for it to happen.

New York City, USA

BUGS AS FOOD

I am sitting in an expensive New York restaurant, and I read the menu. I can't believe my eyes! Chocolate-covered crickets. Wow! I can also order Ant Egg Soup or Silkworm Fried Rice. And it's expensive—$25 for 5 crickets!

I don't like the idea of eating insects. However, in many countries insects are not **luxury** food. They are part of an everyday diet. In Thailand, open-air markets sell silkworms and grasshoppers. Movie theaters in South America sell roasted ants as snacks instead of popcorn.

I am probably eating insects without knowing it, anyway. "It's estimated that the average human eats half a kilogram (1.1 pounds) of insects each year, **unintentionally**," says Lisa Monachelli, director of youth and family programs at New Canaan Nature Center in Connecticut. "For example, in the United States, chocolate can have up to 60 bits of bugs (like legs and heads) per 100 grams. Tomato sauce can contain 30 fly eggs per 100 grams, and peanut butter can have 30 insect bits per 100 grams."

Well, if I am eating insects anyway . . . I decide to order the chocolate-covered crickets, and hey, they taste good.

People eat bugs for food all over the world.

D GOAL 4: Discuss Unusual Foods

rattlesnake

Communication

Many countries have unusual food. At least, it is unusual to visitors to the country. To the people of the country, it is not unusual. In fact, it is often special food—a delicacy. Here are some examples. Do you eat any of these in your country?

Texas, USA	**Rattlesnake**
Mexico	**Ceviche—uncooked fish**
China	**Bird's nest soup**
Scotland	**Haggis—sheep's stomach**
France	**Frog's legs**
Saudi Arabia	**Sheep's eyeballs**

A Write the delicacies in the chart.

I would **definitely** eat this. ☺	I **might** eat this. 😐	I would **never** eat this. ☹

I would never eat haggis.

Fried Rattlesnake

1. Catch and kill a rattlesnake.
2. Remove the skin and intestines.
3. Cut it into 5-cm pieces.
4. Fry it in very hot oil.
5. Eat it!

B Read your answers from the chart to your partner.

C **GOAL CHECK** ✓ **Discuss unusual foods**

Make a list of delicacies that visitors to your country might find unusual. Share it with the class. Answer questions from the class.

Writing

A Write a recipe for one of the delicacies in exercise **C**.

VIDEO JOURNAL: *Dangerous Dinner* E

whale shark

▲ great white shark

▲ stingray

▲ stonefish

▲ pufferfish

Before You Watch

A Work with a partner. Discuss these questions.

1. Which of these fish can kill you?
2. How can they kill you?

While You Watch

A Watch the video. Circle **T** for *true* and **F** for *false*.

1. The pufferfish is not expensive.   T   F
2. Chef Hayashi has a license to prepare *fugu*.   T   F
3. About 30 people die every year because they eat *fugu*.   T   F
4. American General Douglas MacArthur introduced a test for *fugu* chefs.   T   F
5. Tom likes the *fugu*.   T   F

B Answer the questions.

1. Is Tom worried about eating *fugu*? _____
2. When did Chef Hayashi get his license? _____
3. How does *fugu* poison kill a person? _____
4. How many people can a tiger *fugu* kill? _____

After You Watch

A Discuss these questions with a partner.

1. Why do you think people like to eat *fugu*?
2. Would you eat *fugu*?

Food 53

UNIT 5
Sports

British climber Hazel Findlay climbs a sea cliff in Maine, USA.

Look at the photo, answer the questions:

1 What is this sport?

2 What sports do you play? What sports would you like to play?

UNIT 5 GOALS

1. Describe activities happening now
2. Compare everyday and present-time activities
3. Talk about favorite sports
4. Discuss adventures

A GOAL 1: Describe Activities Happening Now

Vocabulary

A Read the conversations. Use the words in blue to label the photos.

Anna is studying for a test. She is bored and tired, so she is calling some friends.

> **Anna:** Hi! What's up? What are you doing?
> **Bridget:** We're at the beach. Kenny's swimming and the others are playing soccer. How about you? What are you doing?
> **Anna:** I'm studying! Grrrr!

> **Anna:** Hi Jill. What are you doing?
> **Jill:** I'm at Eagle Rocks with Antonia and Pete. They're climbing and I'm hiking. It's really cool. Why don't you come?
> **Anna:** I can't. I'm studying for a test.

> **Anna:** Hi Leyla. What's happening?
> **Leyla:** Hi. I'm at the gym. I'm taking a break. Mary and Catalina are here, too. Mary is lifting weights and Catalina is jogging. What are you doing?
> **Anna:** I'm studying. Boring!!!

1. _____

2. _____

3. _____

4. _____

5. _____

6. _____

7. _____

B Take turns. Read the clues to a partner. Guess an activity from exercise **A**. Write your answer.

1. You do this in the gym. _____
2. You do this in a swimming pool. _____
3. You play this with a ball. _____
4. It is like running. _____
5. You do this in the mountains. _____
6. You do this when you are tired. _____

Grammar: Present continuous tense

	Present continuous tense	
Statement	I **am playing** soccer	right now.
Negative	They **are not taking** a break	at the moment.
		now.
Yes/No question	**Are** you **studying**	right now?
		at the moment?
Wh- question	What **are** you **doing**	now?

*We use the present continuous tense to talk about things that are happening at the moment.

A Complete the message. Use the present continuous tense of the verbs given.

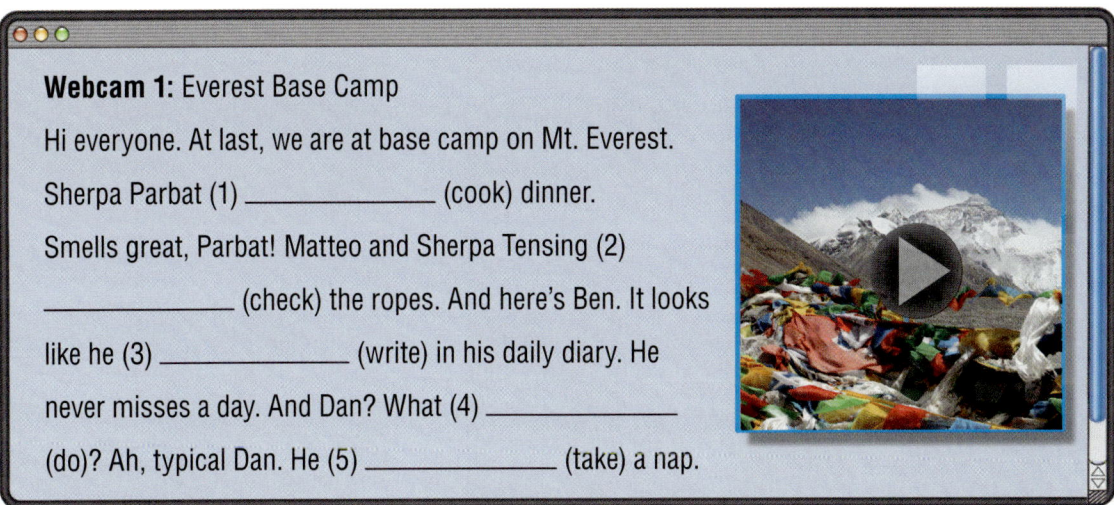

Webcam 1: Everest Base Camp

Hi everyone. At last, we are at base camp on Mt. Everest. Sherpa Parbat (1) _____ (cook) dinner. Smells great, Parbat! Matteo and Sherpa Tensing (2) _____ (check) the ropes. And here's Ben. It looks like he (3) _____ (write) in his daily diary. He never misses a day. And Dan? What (4) _____ (do)? Ah, typical Dan. He (5) _____ (take) a nap.

Conversation

A 🔊 20 Listen to the conversation. What are the twins doing?

Mom: Hey, it's quiet today. Where are the kids?
Dad: Well, Mario's playing basketball in the yard.
Mom: What's Carla doing?
Dad: She's swimming in the pool.
Mom: And the twins? What are they doing?
Dad: Uhh . . . I don't know.
Mom: Hey, you two! What are you doing?
Twins: We're playing soccer!

B Practice the conversation with a partner. Switch roles and practice it again.

C Make a new conversation using other sports.

D **GOAL CHECK** ✓ **Describe activities happening now**

Talk to a partner. What are your family and friends doing now?

Sports 57

B GOAL 2: Compare Everyday and Present-Time Activities

Listening

A 🔊 21 Listen to the phone calls. The people are talking about ____.

a. what they usually do

b. what they are doing at the moment

c. both

▲ go to the movies

▲ go ice skating

▲ study

▲ go to a ball game

▲ play basketball

▲ fix the roof

B 🔊 21 Listen again. What do these people usually do? When?

1. Alan and Karen usually _____ on _____.

2. Khaled usually _____ in the _____.

3. Liam usually _____ on _____.

C 🔊 21 Listen again. What are they doing today?

1. Alan and Karen _____.

2. Khaled _____.

3. Liam _____.

58 Unit 5

▲ A group of boys play volleyball at sunset.

Pronunciation: Reduced form of *What are you . . .*

A 🔊 22 Listen to the full form and the reduced form.

B 🔊 23 Listen and check (✓) the correct column.

	Full form	Reduced form
1. What are you reading?		
2. What are you thinking?		
3. What are you playing?		
4. What are you cooking?		
5. What are you writing?		

C 🔊 23 Listen again. Repeat the sentences.

D Practice this conversation using the reduced form. Repeat the conversation using *eat, read,* and *write*. Replace the underlined words.

A: What are you doing?

B: I'm cooking.

A: What are you cooking?

B: I'm cooking rice.

Communication

A One member of the group mimes a sport. The other members of the group try to guess the sport.

B GOAL CHECK ✓ **Compare everyday and present-time activities**

Work with a partner. What are you doing now? What do you do at this time on a Sunday?

> Are you playing volleyball?

> Yes, I am.

Sports 59

C GOAL 3: Talk About Favorite Sports

Language Expansion: Team sports and individual sports

A Write the following sports in the correct box according to the categories.

baseball   gymnastics   football   volleyball
ice hockey   diving   skateboarding   golf

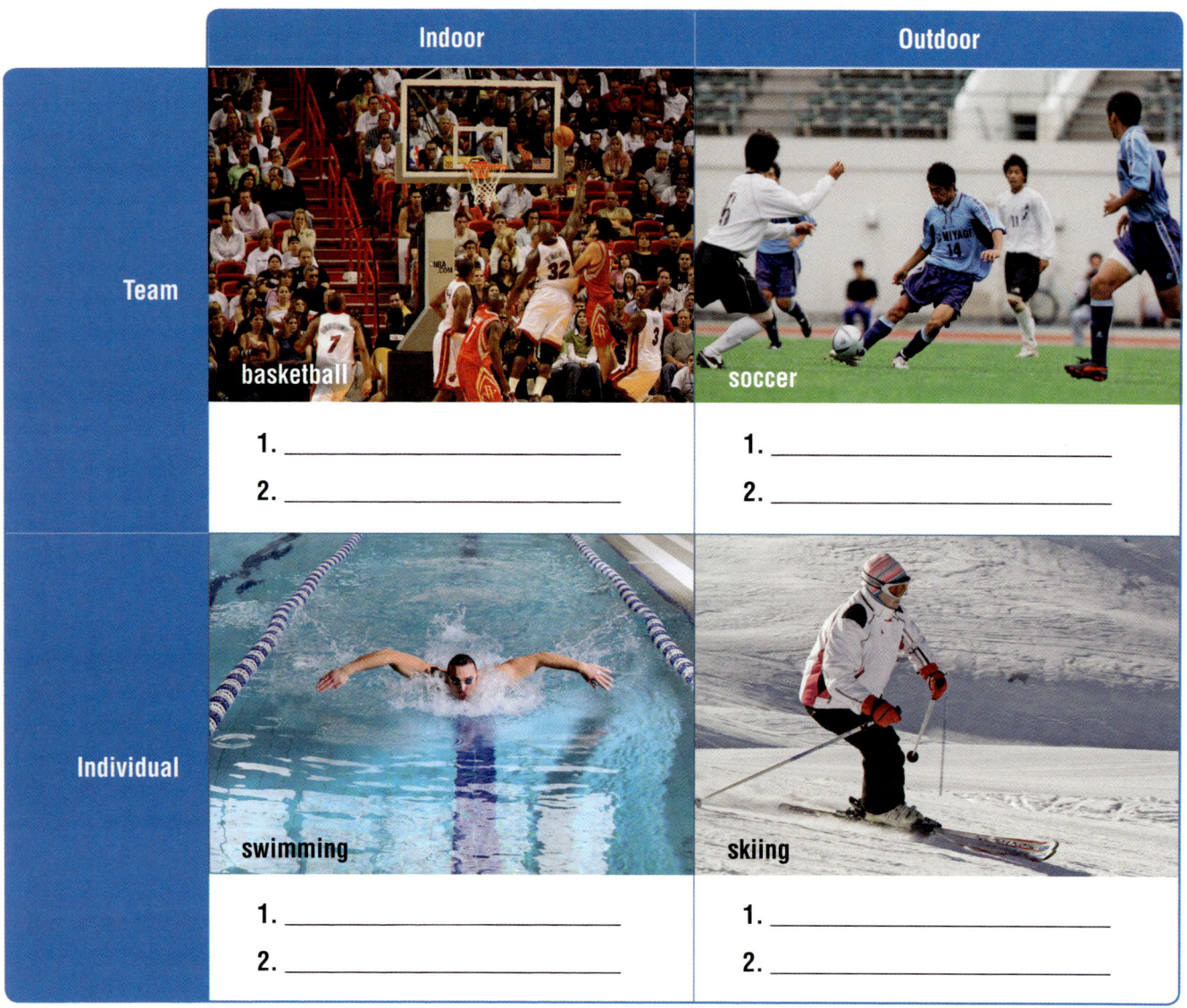

	Indoor	Outdoor
Team	basketball 1. _____ 2. _____	soccer 1. _____ 2. _____
Individual	swimming 1. _____ 2. _____	skiing 1. _____ 2. _____

Word Focus

We use *play* for team games—for example, *I **play** soccer.*

We use *go* for individual sports—for example, *I **go** swimming.*

B Work in groups. Make a chart with new ways to categorize sports. Have the other groups guess the names of your categories.

C Write the names of more sports.

play	soccer,
go	swimming,

60 Unit 5

Grammar: Stative verbs

Stative verbs			
like	Why do you **like** outdoor sports? I **like** to be outdoors.	know	You **know** I can't swim.
hate	I **hate** indoor sports.	want	I don't **want** to go bungee jumping.
think	I **think** indoor sports are boring.	need	You **need** a lot of equipment.
prefer	Do you **prefer** outdoor sports?	cost	The equipment **costs** a lot of money.

*We usually do not use stative verbs in the present continuous tense.

A Circle the correct form of the verb in parentheses.

1. Skiing is expensive. It (is costing | costs) a lot of money.
2. I (am needing | need) a new soccer shirt.
3. The kids (are playing | play) in the garden at the moment.
4. I don't like team games. I (am preferring | prefer) individual sports.

B Write the correct form of the verb in parentheses.

1. Ashira _____ (not like) to go swimming.
2. I _____ (play) golf right now. Can I call you back?
3. I like rock climbing but my friend _____ (hate) it.
4. Frederick can't come. He _____ (fix) the car.

Real Language

We say *me too* to agree with a positive statement and *me neither* to agree with a negative statement.

Conversation

A 🔊 24 Listen to the conversation. Does Adrian want to try rock climbing?

Adrian: Why do you like rock climbing?
Kris: I hate to be indoors all the time.
Adrian: Me too, but it looks dangerous. I don't want to die.
Kris: Me neither! That's why we use ropes.
Adrian: Do you need a lot of equipment?
Kris: Yes, you do, and it costs a lot of money.
Adrian: So it's expensive and dangerous! Well, I think it's a crazy sport. Definitely not for me.

B Practice the conversation with a partner. Switch roles and practice it again. Then change the sport and make a new conversation.

C GOAL CHECK ✓ **Talk about favorite sports**

Tell a partner about your favorite sport. Say why you like it.

Sports 61

D GOAL 4: Discuss Adventures

Reading

A Lewis Pugh is an activist who does remarkable things to call attention to **environmental** problems. Look at the photos. Match what he and his team are doing to the photos.

1. _____ 2. _____

3. _____ 4. _____

a. He is swimming.   c. They are hiking.
b. He is speaking.   d. They are rowing.

B Read the article with a partner. Underline the sentences with stative verbs.

C Circle T for *true* or F for *false*.

1. Lewis Pugh is not a very good swimmer. T F
2. Mt. Everest is the tallest mountain on Earth. T F
3. Lake Imja is at the bottom of Mt. Everest. T F
4. A glacier is really the same thing as a lake. T F
5. Lewis Pugh thinks that people can protect the environment. T F

WORD BANK
environment where we live; what is around us; the air, land, sea
glacier a huge area of moving ice
global warming a rise in the earth's temperature causing the climate to change
melting becoming water because of heat

Lewis Pugh Adventurer/Environmentalist

MY MIND-SHIFTING EVEREST SWIM

The following article is about Lewis Pugh. After Unit 6, you'll have the opportunity to watch some of Pugh's TED Talk and learn more about his idea worth spreading.

Lewis Pugh is a famous swimmer, but not in the way you might think. In 2007 he swam across the North Pole in water that was so cold his fingers were frozen. Why did Pugh do this? Well, he wants people to pay attention to **global warming** and the problems it is causing.

As a boy, Lewis visited national parks and he learned how fragile and amazing the Earth is. Now he wants to protect the Earth and draw attention to the problems facing it. He decided to swim in water near the North Pole to bring attention to the **melting glaciers** and icecap. Lewis said that the swim was so scary and painful that it would be his last time swimming in freezing water. But when he heard about Lake Imja, near Mt. Everest, high in the Himalayas, he decided to swim in cold water again.

Mt. Everest is the tallest mountain in the world and swimming there is very difficult. It's so high that it's hard to breathe. You feel sick and your head hurts. Because of global warming, glaciers on Mt. Everest are melting and leaving lakes behind, like Lake Imja. This means there's less water for people who need it in nearby countries like China, India, Pakistan, and Bangladesh.

Lewis says he learned two lessons from swimming at Mt. Everest. First, he learned that people can unintentionally do a lot of damage. We do things that hurt the Earth because we know no other way to live. Second, he learned that if we change the way we think, we can do things we didn't think were possible. We can all do something to protect our environment if we change the way we think and think more about our future.

"I heard about the Himalayas and the melting of the glaciers because of climate change."

"Very few things are impossible to achieve if we really put our whole minds to it."

– Lewis Pugh

D GOAL 4: Discuss Adventures

A lake created by a melted glacier in the Himalayas

Communication

A Match the equipment to the activity. Write the correct number.

1. a ball   _____ playing soccer
2. boots   _____ ice hockey
3. a bathing suit   _____ hiking
4. a backpack   _____ swimming
5. skates   _____ mountain climbing

B Complete the sentences with the correct verbs. Use the words in the box.

fishing   climbing
swimming jogging

1. We love the water. We are going _____ tomorrow.
2. Ahmed wants to catch and eat some shrimp. He is going _____.
3. They like the mountains. They are going _____ this weekend.
4. Jill would like to exercise in the park. She is going _____ today.

C Lewis Pugh swims in dangerous conditions. What other sports can be dangerous? How are they dangerous? Have you ever played a dangerous sport? Which one? Discuss with a partner.

"We all got down onto the ice, and I then got into my swimming costume and I dived into the sea. I have never in my life felt anything like that moment. I could barely breathe. I was gasping for air."

Writing

A Read Lewis Pugh's quote. Then write an e-mail to a friend about a dangerous sport that you'd like to try.

B GOAL CHECK ✓ **Discuss adventures**

Share your e-mail with a partner. How are they the same? How are they different?

64 Unit 5

VIDEO JOURNAL: Cheese-Rolling Races E

cheese rolling

▲ octopush

▲ sepak takraw

Before You Watch

A Which of these unusual sports would you like to try? Why? Discuss with a partner.

While You Watch

A Fill in the blanks. Use the words in the box. Watch the video and check your answers.

> injuries   cold
> spectators   winner

1. The first _____ of the day is Craig Brown.
2. One year, one of the cheeses went into the _____.
3. It's not just spectators who get injured—competitors do as well, especially when it's _____ or there hasn't been much rain.
4. Cheese-rolling spectator: "It's when the ground is really hard . . . that's when the _____ are going to happen."

After You Watch

A Discuss these questions with a partner.

1. Why do you think people join the cheese-rolling race?
2. Do they want the cheese?
3. Do they want to have fun?
4. Are they crazy?

Communication

A Role-play the following situation.

Student A is a competitor in the cheese-rolling race.

Student B interviews him or her.

> Why do you come?

> Where do you come from?

Sports 65

UNIT 6
Destinations

Angkor in Cambodia was a "lost" city, but now the ruins are a tourist destination and World Heritage site.

Look at the photo, answer the questions:

1. Do you know the name of this place? Where is it?
2. Do you enjoy traveling? Why?

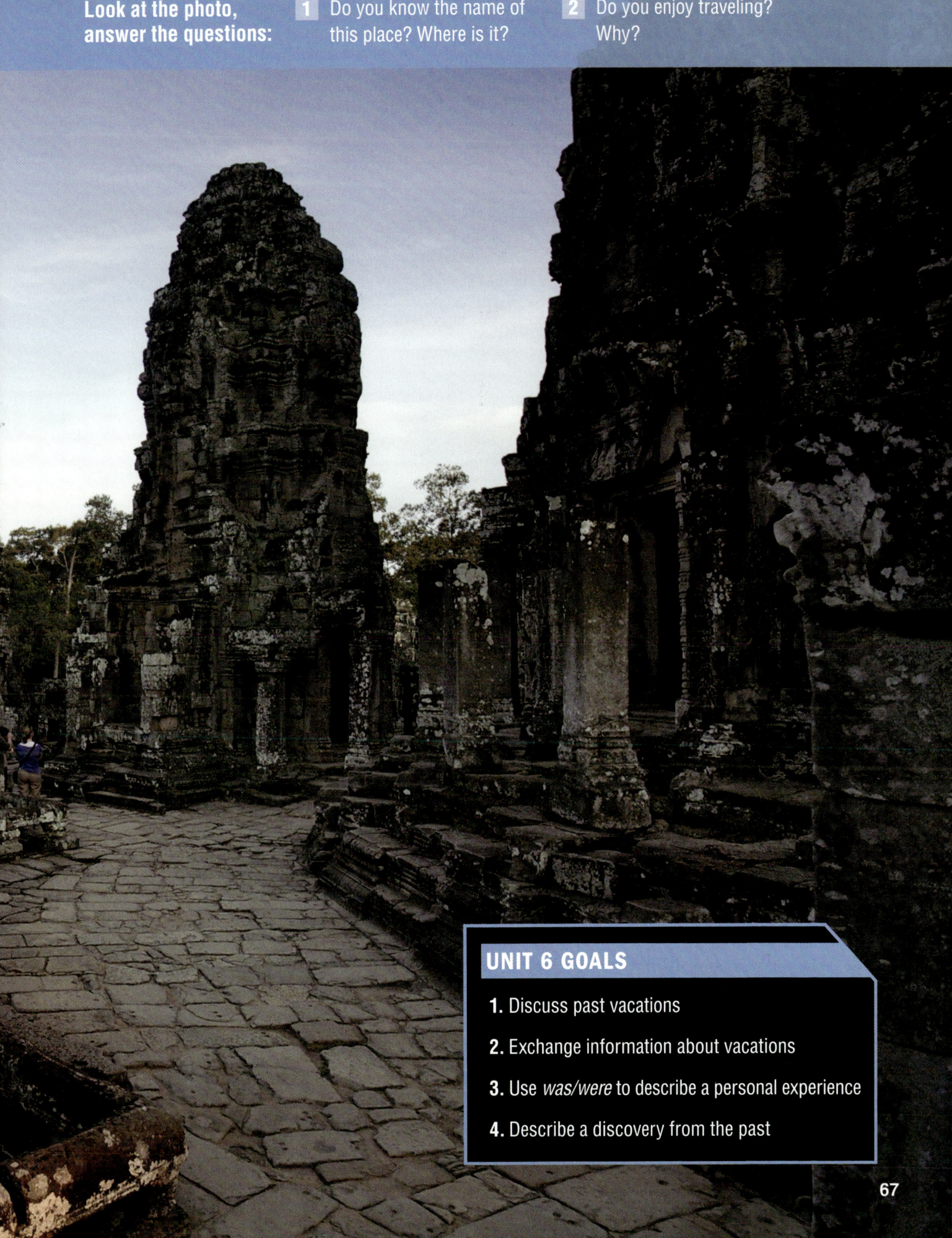

UNIT 6 GOALS

1. Discuss past vacations
2. Exchange information about vacations
3. Use *was/were* to describe a personal experience
4. Describe a discovery from the past

A GOAL 1: Discuss Past Vacations

Vocabulary

visit places of interest ____
take a bus tour ____
check into the hotel ____
rent a car ____
take photos ____
pack/unpack suitcases ____
buy souvenirs ____

A Match the photos to an action from the box. Write the numbers.

1

2

3

4

5

6

7

B Which of these activities do you do *before* and *during* your vacation?

Before	During

C Write other things you do before and during a vacation. Share your ideas with the class.

Grammar: Simple past tense

Simple past tense	
Statement	He **rented** a car on his trip to Europe last November.
Negative	I **didn't have** a reservation yesterday.
Yes/No questions	**Did** they **go** to Asia last year?
Short answers	Yes, they **did**./No, they **didn't**.
Information questions	Where **did** you **go** for your vacation last year?

*We use the simple past tense to talk about completed actions or conditions.

*Some verbs are regular in the simple past tense. They have an *-ed* ending.		*Some verbs are irregular in the simple past tense. They have many different forms.	
learn — learned	travel — traveled	eat — ate	tell — told
arrive — arrived	want — wanted	buy — bought	leave — left
play — played	need — needed	fly — flew	say — said
ask — asked	help — helped	know — knew	see — saw
		go — went	take — took

A Unscramble the questions and answers. Use your notebook.

1. **Q:** to Europe Did you go year? last
   A: to we No, went America.

2. **Q:** did buy you those Where souvenirs?
   A: them bought in We Boston.

68   Unit 6

B Fill in the blanks using the simple past tense of the words in parentheses.

Normally we go to Spain for our vacation, but this year we (1) _____ (not go). Instead, we (2) _____ (decide) to go somewhere different, and we (3) _____ (choose) Dubai in the United Arab Emirates. We (4) _____ (stay) at the Burj Al Arab hotel – "The Best Hotel in the Middle East." There are nine restaurants in the hotel, but we (5) _____ (not eat) in all the restaurants. And of course, the shopping was fantastic. We (6) _____ (buy) lots of clothes and a few souvenirs. We also (7) _____ (rent) a car and (8) _____ (go) to the desert. It is really beautiful, and we (9) _____ (take) hundreds of photos. It was an excellent vacation.

Conversation

A 25 Listen to the conversation. How long did Maria stay in Venice?

Christine: Hey, I love that scarf, Maria. Where did you buy it?
Maria: I bought it in Italy. We went to Italy for our vacation last year.
Christine: Wow! Sounds cool. Did you go to Rome?
Maria: No, we flew directly to Venice. I wanted to see the Doge's Palace.
Christine: How long did you stay there?
Maria: We stayed for five nights.
Christine: Lucky you!

B Practice the conversation with a partner. Switch roles and practice it again.

C Practice the conversation again and change the underlined words. You can use the information in the chart to help you, or use your own ideas.

Country	Italy	United States	Great Britain
Capital	Rome	Washington, D.C.	London
Other city	Venice	Orlando	Edinburgh
Place of special interest	Doge's Palace	Disney World	The Castle

D GOAL CHECK ✓ **Discuss past vacations**

Take turns with a partner talking about a vacation you took.

▲ The Burj Al Arab hotel in Dubai

B GOAL 2: Exchange Information About Vacations

Listening

A 🔊 26 Listen to the conversation. Circle the correct answer.

1. Chen is telling his friend about _____.
   a. his vacation   b. his hobby   c. his work

2. His friend is _____.
   a. bored   b. interested   c. tired

B 🔊 26 Listen again. Circle **T** for *true* or **F** for *false*. Correct the false statements in your notebook.

1. Chen went to Oklahoma.   T F
2. He visited five theme parks.   T F
3. He didn't like Sea World.   T F
4. He went to the Spider-Man™ ride.   T F
5. He visited Islands of Adventure.   T F
6. He didn't try the Incredible Hulk Coaster. T F

Pronunciation: Sounds of *-ed* endings

A 🔊 27 Listen. Check (✓) the correct boxes in the chart to the left. Then listen again and repeat.

	/t/	/d/	/ɪd/
packed	✓		
traveled		✓	
wanted			✓
arrived			
played			
needed			
asked			
helped			
visited			
rented			
liked			

B 🔊 28 Listen to the sentences and check (✓) the pronunciation of the *-ed* ending.

	/d/	/t/	/ɪd/
We **checked** into the hotel.			
I **packed** my bags.			
He **traveled** to Europe.			
They **stayed** at an expensive hotel.			

C 🔊 28 Listen again and repeat the sentences.

Communication

A 🔄 Read the travel blogs on the next page. Fill in the gaps with the past tense of the verbs in parentheses.

70 Unit 6

From Zanzibar to Zebras
Africa » Tanzania » Dar es Salaam » Zamzibar » Arusha

Read full story | Subscribe

December 12th, 2014

Day 1 __Arrived__ (arrive) in Dar es Salaam. _____ (check) into hotel. _____ (unpack) suitcases. Went swimming.

Day 2 _____ (take) boat to the island of Zanzibar.

Days 3–5 _____ (sunbathe) on the beach. _____ (go) diving.

Day 6 _____ (fly) to Arusha. Saw Kilimanjaro. It's BIG!

Days 7–10 _____ (take) a safari tour. _____ (see) hundreds of wild animals. Took lots of photos.

Day 11 _____ (return) to Arusha. _____ (buy) souvenirs. Took plane to Dar es Salaam and then flew home. Great trip.

Mexico: Beaches and Pyramids
Mexico » Mexico City » Cancun » Tulum » Merida

Read full story | Subscribe

December 18th, 2014

Day 1 __Arrived__ (arrive) in Mexico City. _____ (take) subway to Chapultepec Park. _____ (go) to zoo.

Day 2 _____ (rent) a car. _____ (visit) the Pyramid of the Sun.

Days 3–5 _____ (fly) to Cancun. _____ (go) to the beach.

Day 6 Visited ruins at Tulum. _____ (watch) traditional dance show.

Day 7 Colonial city of Merida. Took a bus tour of the city. _____ (drink) hot chocolate in market.

Day 8 _____ (return) to Mexico City. Flew home.

B Choose one blog. Take turns with a partner asking each other questions about your vacation.

- Where did you go next?
- What did you do?
- How long did you stay there?
- Did you enjoy it? Why?

C **GOAL CHECK** ✓ **Exchange information about vacations**

Join another pair of students. Tell them about your partner's vacation from the activity above.

---

fly – flew   sunbathe – sunbathed
watch – watched   drink – drank

Destinations 71

C GOAL 3: Use *Was/Were* to Describe a Personal Experience

Adjectives	Emphatic adjectives
good/nice	excellent outstanding magnificent amazing
bad	awful terrible horrible
interesting	fascinating
tiring	exhausting
dirty	filthy
clean	spotless
big	enormous huge

Language Expansion: Emphatic adjectives

A Write two or three emphatic adjectives below each picture.

_____   _____

_____   _____

B Use emphatic adjectives to complete the text.

We had an (1) _____ vacation. We visited six European countries in six days. My favorite country was Italy. Rome is a (2) _____ city. There is so much to see: museums, churches, ruins. We stayed in a (3) _____ hotel. Everything about it was perfect. It had an (4) _____ swimming pool and very friendly people.

Grammar: Simple past tense of *to be*

Simple past tense of *to be*	
Statement	I **was** exhausted.
Negative	The food **wasn't** great.
Information questions	Why **was** your vacation awful?
Yes/No questions	**Were** they tired?
Short answers	No, they **weren't**.

A Match the questions and the answers.

1. Were you tired? _____
2. Where were they? _____
3. Was the weather good? _____
4. Was he late? _____
5. Were the rooms clean? _____

a. No, he wasn't. He was on time.
b. They were in Peru.
c. No, they weren't. They were filthy.
d. Yes, I was. I was exhausted.
e. Yes, it was. It was excellent.

B Complete the sentences with *was* or *were*.

1. We didn't enjoy our vacation. The weather _____ very bad.
2. How _____ the food?
3. _____ you tired when you got home?
4. I _____ really interested in the ruins. They were amazing.
5. _____ the hotel clean?

C Complete the sentences with the correct forms of *to be*.

Last year we went diving at Pulau Sipadan, Malaysia. It (1) _____ amazing! There (2) _____ lots of turtles, and we saw some hammerhead sharks, as well. We also went to Barracuda Point, but unfortunately, there (3) _____ any barracuda. It (4) _____ the wrong time of year. We stayed at the Dive Center and the food (5) _____ excellent. The rooms (6) _____ spotless.

▲ A diver in Pulau Sipadan

D Write three questions about exercise **C** to ask your partner.

Conversation

A 🔊 29 Listen to the conversation. What was good about the vacation?

Alex: How was your vacation?
Mike: It was terrible.
Alex: Why? What happened?
Mike: Well, first of all, the weather was <u>bad</u>. It rained nonstop for two weeks.
Alex: Oh, no.
Mike: And the hotel was <u>dirty</u>. It was full of cockroaches.
Alex: Yuck! And how was the food?
Mike: Actually, the food was <u>good</u>.
Alex: Well, at least you enjoyed something.
Mike: Not really. I had a bad stomach and couldn't eat. Some vacation!

B Practice the conversation with a partner. Switch roles and practice it again.

C Practice again and change the underlined adjectives to emphatic adjectives.

D **GOAL CHECK** ✓ Use *was/were* to describe a personal experience

Tell a partner about a good or bad experience you had.

The weather was awful.

The food was excellent.

Destinations 73

D GOAL 4: Describe a Discovery from the Past

Reading

A Look at the black and white photos. When do you think these photos were taken?

B Read the article. Underline the emphatic adjectives.

C Underline the regular simple past verbs and circle the irregulars.

D Answer the questions.

1. Did Hiram Bingham discover Inca ruins in Ollantaytambo? _____

2. How much did he pay Arteaga? _____

3. Was the climb to Machu Picchu easy? _____

4. Where did they eat? _____

▲ A man stands at the walls of the main temple.

Word Focus
hut = a small house
ruins = old buildings that have fallen down
to clear = to cut down

Machu Picchu, Peru

THE CRADLE OF THE INCA EMPIRE

Photograph of Machu Picchu taken by Hiram Bingham

Most people travel for vacations, but some people travel to explore and discover new places. In 1911, Hiram Bingham, an American archaeologist, traveled to Peru where he discovered Machu Picchu, the lost city of the Incas. Read his report of the discovery.

In 1911, I went to Cuzco in Peru looking for ancient Inca **ruins.** We left Cuzco and traveled to the modern city of Urubamba. We then continued down the Urubamba River until we came to the beautiful little town of Ollantaytambo. We continued down the river, and six days after we left Cuzco, we arrived at a place called Mandorpampa. A man came and introduced himself as Arteaga, and I asked him about ruins. He told us of some ruins in the mountains, called Machu Picchu. I offered to pay him 50 cents per day to take us to the ruins, and he agreed.

The next day, we crossed the river and began an exhausting climb. At noon we arrived at a little grass **hut.** The people there were very friendly and gave us some boiled potatoes and cool water. The view was magnificent, the water was delicious, but there were no ruins. However, we continued upward until at last we arrived on top of the mountain. Immediately, we found some ancient Inca walls made of white stone. I knew at once that this was a truly amazing discovery.

I returned to Machu Picchu in 1912, and we began **to clear** the forest. We started to see the ruins, and they were outstanding. The walls are made from enormous stones, and as we continued to clear the forest, we discovered more and more ruins. At last, the lost city of Machu Picchu appeared before us.

Destinations 75

D GOAL 4: Describe a Discovery from the Past

The Pyramids of Giza

Communication

A Work with a group and fill in as much information in the chart as you can.

	Stonehenge	Pyramids of Giza	A ruin in your country
Where is it?	in England		
What was it?	a burial ground		
Who built it?	Ancient Britons		
When was it built?	3000 BCE–2000 BCE		

B Share your information with the class and write in any new information from classmates.

Writing

A Write a travel blog about one of the places from the chart. Use your notebook for extra space if needed.

_____

_____

_____

_____

B GOAL CHECK ✓ **Describe a discovery from the past**

Talk to a partner about a discovery from the past that you know about.

VIDEO JOURNAL: Machu Picchu   E

Before You Watch

A Fill in the blanks. Use the words in the box to complete the video summary.

> tourists environment
> quiet business

Video summary

When Hiram Bingham discovered Machu Picchu, it was a (1) _____ place. Now, many (2) _____ go to Machu Picchu every day. Some people say it is good for (3) _____, but other people say it is bad for the (4) _____.

While You Watch

A Watch the video. Circle **T** for *true* and **F** for *false*.

1. Machu Picchu is a popular tourist destination. **T F**
2. Machu Picchu is sometimes known as the Lost Town of the Incas. **T F**
3. Conservationists think tourism is good for Machu Picchu. **T F**
4. Jose wants more people to come to Machu Picchu. **T F**

After You Watch

A Discuss these questions with a partner.

1. What are the big tourist attractions in your country?
2. Are there any problems with tourism in your country? What are they?
3. Do you think tourism is good or bad? Give reasons.

> **Tourists buy souvenirs and stay in hotels.**

> **That's good. It brings money to the country.**

Destinations 77

TEDTALKS

Lewis Pugh Adventurer/Environmentalist
MY MIND-SHIFTING EVEREST SWIM

Before You Watch

A Look at the pictures. Which of these places would you like to visit? Why? Research the places if needed. Tell a partner. Do you share the same answers?

Greenland

Patagonia, Chile

Mt. Everest, Nepal

Santa Cruz, Argentina

B Use the words in the box to complete the TED Talk summary.

| symbolic | humility | aggressive |
| Sherpas | debrief | sustainable |

WORD BANK
aggressive to do something with a lot of force
battleground a place where there are a lot of problems or conflict
debrief to talk about something after it is done
humility thinking you are not more important than other people or things
instability a situation that can change at any time
Sherpas people who live in the Himalayas and work as mountain guides
sustainable something that will last a long time
symbolic representing something
tactical something that is smartly planned

Lewis Pugh's idea worth spreading is that we can do something to stop climate change; we just need to take it seriously. That's why he swam across Lake Imja, a place that should be made of ice. Watch Pugh's full TED Talk at TED.com.

TED Talk Summary

Lewis Pugh swims in cold places because it is _____ of saving the environment. He wants Earth to be _____, or around forever. Lewis decided to swim in a lake high on Mt. Everest in the Himalayas. _____ helped him climb the big mountain to Lake Imja. After a failed first attempt, Lewis had a _____ to discuss the best way to swim at 5,300 meters (17,400 feet) above sea level. He is usually very _____ when he swims because he wants to finish quickly and get out of the cold water. But this time he showed _____ and swam slowly.

C Look closely at the pictures in exercise **A** again. All of these places used to be completely covered in snow and ice. Discuss the following questions as a group.

What do you think is happening to the snow and ice in the pictures? Why? What do you think you will see in the TED Talk?

While You Watch

A Watch the TED Talk. Put the quotes in order. Write the number in the boxes provided.

78

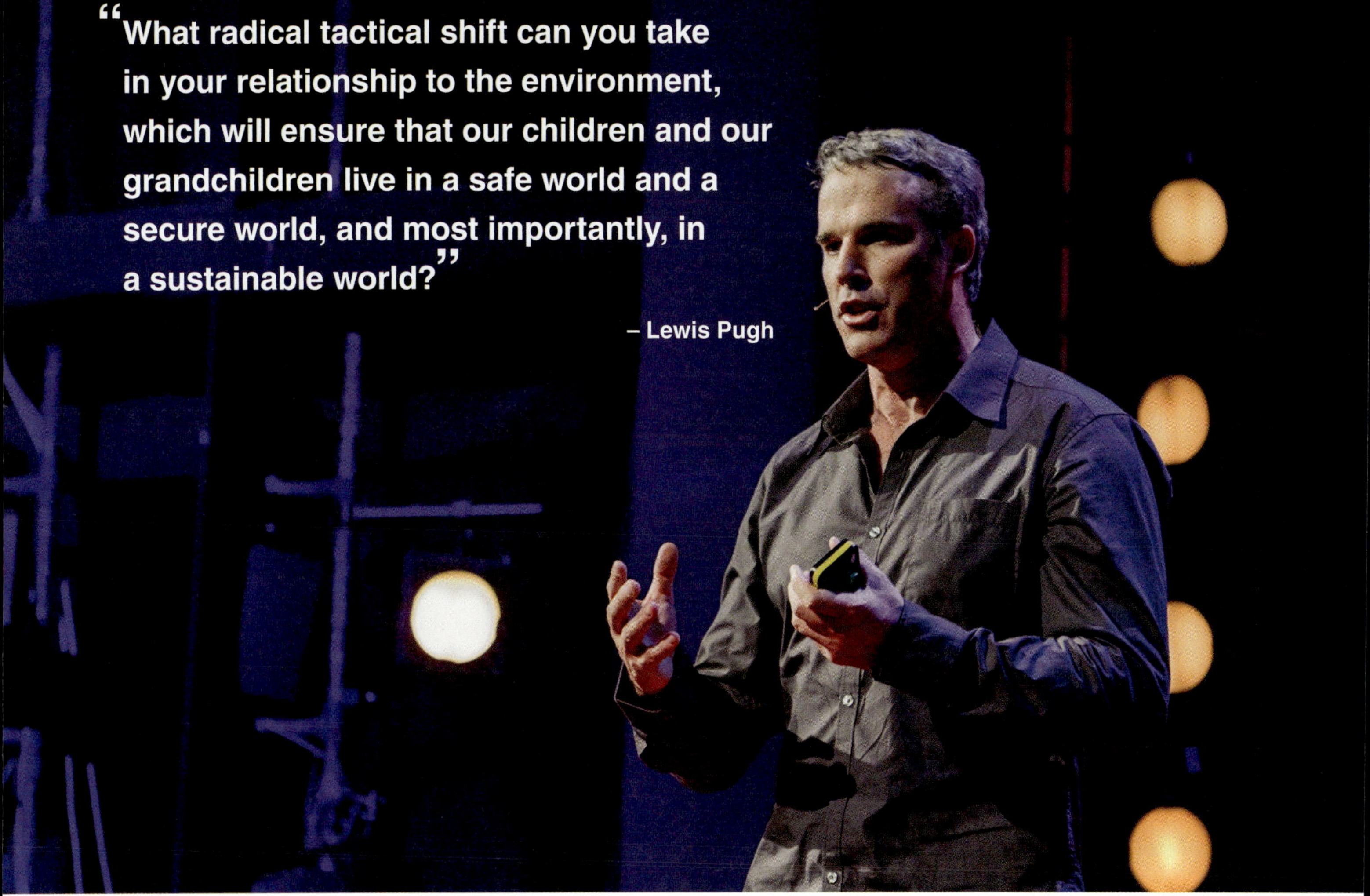

"What radical tactical shift can you take in your relationship to the environment, which will ensure that our children and our grandchildren live in a safe world and a secure world, and most importantly, in a sustainable world?"

– Lewis Pugh

"And I remember getting out of the water and my hands feeling so painful and looking down at my fingers, and my fingers were literally the size of sausages."

"I heard about this lake, Lake Imja. This lake has been formed in the last couple of years because of the melting of the glacier."

"And so I decided to walk up to Mt. Everest, the highest mountain on this earth, and go and do a symbolic swim underneath the summit of Mt. Everest."

"And I swam across the lake. And I can't begin to tell you how good I felt when I came to the other side."

TEDTALKS

Lewis Pugh Adventurer/Environmentalist
MY MIND-SHIFTING EVEREST SWIM

After You Watch

A Watch the TED Talk again. Circle the correct answer for each question.

1. What are the Himalayas?	big lakes	big mountains
2. How long did Lewis swim at the North Pole?	19 minutes	30 minutes
3. What is melting in the Himalayas?	glaciers	lakes
4. How many people depend on water from the Himalayas?	2 billion	1 million
5. What is the world's population?	9 billion	6.8 billion

B Fill in the names of the places from the words in the box.

> Lake Imja   North Pole   Bangladesh
> Mt. Everest   Himalayas

1. In 2007, Lewis Pugh swam at the _____ .
2. The glaciers in the _____ are melting.
3. The highest mountain on Earth is _____ .
4. _____ is very high, near the top of Mt. Everest.
5. China, India, Pakistan, and _____ are countries near the Himalayas.

C Use the emphatic adjectives to complete the sentences.

> exhausting   fascinating   enormous
> excellent   awful

1. Mt. Everest isn't small. It's a(n) _____ mountain.
2. His story wasn't boring. It was _____ .
3. Lewis Pugh survived his North Pole swim. He must be a(n) _____ swimmer.
4. Swimming for a very long time, especially in cold conditions, isn't easy. It is _____ .
5. When Lewis Pugh first tried the swim, he had to stop. He felt _____ .

A melting ice field

D Lewis Pugh completed his amazing swims to call attention to the problem of global warming. Here are some things caused by global warming. Write the correct captions under the pictures. Have you seen any of these things before? Give examples and discuss with a partner.

Effects of Global Warming

| Animals in Danger | Huge Storms |
| No Water | Floods |

1. _____ 2. _____

3. _____ 4. _____

E Make a list of things of things you can do to protect the environment. Discuss as a group. Share your list with other groups.

Challenge! Look at the pictures from exercise **D** again. Research other effects of global warming. Make a list. Then research what your country is doing to address the problem of global warming. Is it enough? Write an essay with your ideas to share with the class.

GLOSSARY

UNIT 1

boring: not interesting
chef: a cook in a restaurant
dancer: a person who earns money by dancing
dangerous: unsafe or harmful
doctor: a professional who helps sick or injured people
engineer: a person who plans the making of machines, roads, and bridges
happy: a joyful or cheerful feeling
interesting: something that is exciting or unusual
journalist: a person whose job is to collect news
photographer: someone who takes photos as a job
pilot: a professional who flies airplanes
police officer: a person who is trained to maintain law and order
politician: a person with a job in politics or government
poor: to not have a lot of money
rich: to have a lot of money
teacher: a person whose job is to instruct and educate others
travel agent: a person who plans trips and holidays
safe: not harmful or dangerous
unhappy: a sad feeling

UNIT 2

brush your teeth: clean your teeth with a small brush
catch the bus: get on a bus on time
celebrate: to do something special, like have a party, to mark an occasion
costumes: clothes worn by a person who is trying to look like a different person or thing
decorate: to make a place or object look beautiful or festive
eat breakfast: eat the first meal of the day, usually in the morning
eat out: eat at a restaurant
festival: a public celebration that takes place on special occasions
fireworks: colorful explosions of light in the sky, usually used for celebrations
fun: a good time
get up: wake up and get out of bed
go to bed: lie down to go to sleep
go to the movies: go to a theater to watch a film
masks: material worn on the face to hide one's identity
present: a gift
start work: begin your job
take a nap: sleep for a short time when it is not time for bed
take a shower: wash under a shower
watch TV: look at a TV
visit friends: go see friends

UNIT 3

airline ticket: a printed piece of paper bought for travel on an airplane
board the airplane: get on the airplane
buy duty free goods: buy goods at a store in an airport that do not add tax to the price
buy your ticket: use cash or credit cards to get a ticket
cash: paper money, like dollar bills, and metal coins used to buy things
check in: arrive and show your ticket
credit cards: a plastic card that allows a person to buy things by borrowing money
claim your baggage: pick up bags or suitcases after a flight
go through customs: when items brought into a country are checked by an official
go through immigration: have government workers check the passports and visas of travelers
go through security: have government workers check travelers to make sure no one has anything dangerous
international driver's license: a document that allows people to drive a car or motorcycle in foreign countries
pack your bags: put clothes and other things in bags
passport: a small book issued by a government to a citizen of a nation for travel
take a taxi: get somewhere using a car with a driver for hire
travel insurance: an agreement with a company in which you pay them money to cover costs and reduce the risk of travel
visa: a document that allows a person to travel to a country

UNIT 4

apple: a round fruit with firm, white flesh
bagel: a piece of bread that is round with a hole in the middle
banana: a long, curved fruit with yellow skin
beans: seeds that can be eaten
breakfast cereal: a breakfast food made from grain
broccoli: a vegetable with green stalks and green or purple heads
butter: soft yellow substance made from cream
cauliflower: large, round vegetable with a hard, white center
cheese: a solid food made from milk
chicken: the meat from a type of farm bird
coffee: a hot, brown, energy-giving drink made by water and coffee beans
customer: someone who buys goods or services
dairy products: different types of food that are made from milk
drinks: liquids that can be swallowed
egg: oval object made by birds, often eaten as food
fiber: a part of a plant found in many fruits and vegetables that is a part of a healthy diet
fish: the meat from an animal with fins that lives in the sea
fruits: the part of a plant that holds the seeds
hamburger: ground meat shaped into a flat circle
juice: a liquid that comes from a fruit or vegetable
lemon: a bright yellow fruit with sour juice
lettuce: a vegetable with large green leaves
meat: the flesh of animals
milk: a white liquid produced by some female animals such as cows
nuts: a fruit with a hard shell or its seed
onion: a round, layered vegetable with light brown skin
orange: a round juicy fruit with orange skin
pepper: a hollow vegetable with seeds inside
potato: round vegetables with white or red skins and white insides
protein: a substance found in meat, fish, and dairy foods that promotes growth
sausage: meat formed into a tube
shrimp: small shellfish with long tails
soda: a sweet carbonated drink
steak: a large piece of meat or fish
tea: flowers and leaves that are dried, shredded, and brewed into a drink
tomato: a soft, red fruit
tuna salad: a food that has chopped tuna meat and vegetables
turkey bacon: salted and smoked turkey meat
vegetables: different plants that can be eaten as food
waiter: a person who serves food and drink in a restaurant
water: clear liquid with no color or taste, people and animals need it to survive

UNIT 5

baseball: a game played on a field by nine players on each team using a small ball and a bat
climbing: a sport where a person moves upward over a vertical surface
diving: a water sport where a person jumps into water
fix the roof: repair the top of a house
football: a sport played by two 11-person teams, using an oval ball. In order to win one must pass or run the ball over the opponent's line
golf: an outdoors game in which people hit a small hard ball into a hole with a stick
go to the movies: (see Unit 2)
gymnastics: exercises that develop strength, coordination, and movement
hiking: taking a long walk in the country or up a mountain
ice hockey: ice-skating sport that uses curved sticks and a small round disk
jogging: running slowly as a form of exercise
lifting weights: a sport in which people try to lift very heavy objects
playing soccer: play a sport of two teams of 11 players, who kick a round ball into goals
skateboarding: a sport where people do tricks on a narrow board with four wheels
study: spend time learning about a subject
swimming: a sport in which people move through water by moving parts of the body
taking a break: taking time to relax
volleyball: a sport played with six players on each side of a net who score points by grounding the ball on the opponents' side

UNIT 6

buy souvenirs: buy objects to remember a place
check into the hotel: arrive at a hotel and get a room
emphatic adjectives: (See page 72)
pack suitcases: to place objects in bags or luggage in order to transport them during travel
unpack suitcases: to remove objects from a bag or luggage
rent a car: to pay money in order to use a car
take a bus tour: go on a bus that will visit places of interest and have a guide
take photos: take pictures with a camera
visit places of interest: go to famous places

UNIT 7

bad: unpleasant or harmful
dirty: not clean
e-mail: mail sent over the Internet
fax: a document that is sent electronically through telephone lines
green: the color of grass
hearing: listening to sounds through the ears
letter: a written or typed message sent by mail
loud: intense sound
newspaper ad: a printed advertisement that appears in a newspaper
salty: something that has the taste of salt
sight: the ability to see using your eyes
smartphone: a mobile phone that can access the Internet
smell: the feeling sensed through the nose
social media: websites and applications used for connecting with people on the Internet
soft: nice to touch
sweet: having a taste like sugar or honey
taste: the sense of flavor that comes from the tongue
text message: an electronic message sent through a cellular phone
touch: the ability to feel through the skin, especially with the fingers
TV: box-like device that shows pictures and sounds
wet: covered with, or full of, water or another liquid

UNIT 8

buy a new car: pay money to own a car
buy my own house: pay money to own a house
clean the house: to remove dirt and dust from a house
cloudy/overcast: covered with clouds; not sunny
cold/cool: having a low temperature; not warm
do the laundry: wash dirty clothes
get a new job: switch jobs
have children: start a family
hot/warm: having a high temperature; not cold
rain boots: shoes that are worn in the rain, usually made out of rubber or plastic
raincoat: a coat that stops a person from getting wet
rainy/wet: having a lot of rain
scarf: a piece of cloth worn around the neck
speak English fluently: to easily speak or write English
study for the next test: practice, read, and listen to get ready for a quiz
sun hat: a hat that protects the head and neck from the sun
sunglasses: eyeglasses that protect the eyes from the sun
sunny/bright/clear: brightly lit with sunlight; not cloudy
sweater: a warm piece of clothing worn over the upper body
swimsuit: a piece of clothing that is worn to go swimming
umbrella: a folding fabric used to protect someone from rain
windy/breezy: with a lot of wind

UNIT 9

belt: a strip of leather or cloth worn around the waist
blouse: a woman's shirt
cheap: goods that don't cost a lot
coat: warm clothing worn over other clothes
cool: a temperature that is low, but not too low
cotton: cloth made from the soft white fiber of a certain plant
expensive: costs a lot of money
gloves: a covering for the hand with separate parts for each finger
handbag: a woman's purse
hat: a clothing item which covers the head
heavy: something that weighs a lot; warm clothing
jacket: a short coat
jeans: informal pants made of denim
leather: animal skin used for clothing
light: something that does not weight a lot; clothing that is not warm
man-made fiber: fibers that are created by people
pants: a piece of clothing that covers the legs
rough: uneven and not smooth
shirt: a piece of clothing worn on the upper body
shoes: a covering for the foot
silk: cloth made from the fibers created by silkworms
skirt: a piece of women's clothing that covers the waist, hips, and part of the legs
smooth: with no roughness or holes
sneakers: a kind of shoe usually worn for sports or casual activities
socks: a piece of cloth worn over the foot and under a shoe
suit: a formal jacket and pants made from the same fabric
tie: a piece of cloth worn by men around the neck for formal occasions
t-shirt: a short-sleeved shirt worn over the upper body
warmth: amount of heat something makes
wool: cloth that is made from sheep's hair

UNIT 10

bad shape: not healthy and physically fit
cycling: to ride on a bicycle
eating a balanced diet: eating all of the important food groups
eating lots of sugar: eating foods and drinks that are sweet and unhealthy
good shape: healthy and physically fit
healthy: in good condition; strong, fit, in good shape
heartwarming: something that makes you happy
homegrown: produced in your own garden
homemade: not made in a factory
junk food: food that tastes good but is bad for your health
lifelong: all your life
lifestyle: a way of living
low calorie: not high in calories
mouth-watering: delicious; very good food
overworked: works too much
smoking: the use of tobacco, usually with cigarettes and cigars
stress-free: without worries or problems
sunbathing: to lie out underneath the sun
works out: exercises
watching lots of TV: spend a lot of time watching TV

UNIT 11

buy the groceries: purchase food and household things
cut the grass: use a machine to shorten grass
get a credit card: sign up for and receive a credit card
get a promotion: receive an advancement to a new and better job
graduate from high school/college: to receive a degree from an academic institution
iron the clothes: smooth out wrinkles on clothing
pass your driving test: pass an examination given to test a person's ability to drive
pay the bills: pay money for heat, electricity, and other household needs
put away the clothes: clean up and store clothes
run a marathon: run a race of over 26 miles (41.3 km)
sweep the floor: to clear a surface of dust or dirt using a broom or brush
travel abroad: travel out of the country
vacuum: to clean with a vacuum cleaner
walk the dog: to take a dog outside

UNIT 12

borrow: to receive something with the promise to return it
budget: an amount of money set aside for a purpose; a financial plan
camel: a large four-legged animal with a long neck and hump(s) on its back
coral reef: hard substance formed from the bones of tiny sea animals
desert: a very dry region with little or no rain
elephant: one of the largest land-mammals, with gray skin, a trunk, and long tusks
expenses: things that must be paid
grasslands: flat land covered with wild grass
income: the amount of money earned from working
interest rates: extra money that has to be paid back when you borrow money
lend: to allow the use of something for a period of time
monkey: a primate with thumbs, long tails, and human-like faces
mountain goat: a four-legged animal with horns that lives on mountains
mountains: a tall formation of land and rock higher than a hill
overspend: to spend too much money
rain forest: a forest with a lot of rainfall that has many different kinds of plants and animals
save: not to spend or use too much money in order to keep some for the future
shark: a meat-eating fish that lives in oceans and large rivers

Glossary 163

SKILLS INDEX

COMMUNICATION
See also **Listening; Speaking; Writing**
- blogs, 71
- contact information, 87
- explaining a choice, 36
- icons, 92
- list-making, 12
- miming, 59
- plan a trip, 151
- role-play, 7, 37, 47, 65, 105, 116

GRAMMAR
- adjectives
  - *be* + adjective (+ noun), 8–9
  - comparatives, 109
  - compound, 128
  - descriptive, 8
  - emphatic, 72
  - possessive, 9, 29
  - superlatives, 112–113
- adverbs of frequency, 21
- *belong to*, 29
- contractions of *be*, 5
- *have to*, 125
- *how much* and *how many* with quantifiers: *lots of*, *a few*, *a little*, 49
- modals (*could, ought to, should, must*), 125
- nouns
  - count and non-count, 44–45
  - possessive, 9
- possessive pronouns, 29
- prepositions of time, 17
- questions with *how*, 128–129
- real conditionals (or first conditional), 148–149, 152–153
- *should* for advice, 33
- *some* and *any*, 44–45
- verbs
  - *be*, 5, 8–9, 72–73
  - future—*be going to*, 96–97, 100–101
  - future tense, 148, 152
  - irregular past tense, 85
  - linking, 88–89
  - present continuous tense, 57
  - present perfect tense, 136–137
  - present perfect tense vs. past simple tense, 140–141
  - simple past tense, 68–69, 72–73
  - simple present tense, 17, 148, 152
  - stative, 61
  - *was/were*, 72–73
  - *will* for predictions and immediate decisions, 100–101
  - *will* in real conditionals, 148–149, 152–153
  - verbs with direct and indirect objects, 84–85

LISTENING
See also **Pronunciation**
- conversations, 5, 9, 17, 21, 29, 30, 33, 45, 49, 57, 61, 69, 70, 73, 85, 89, 97, 101, 109, 110, 113, 125, 129, 137, 141, 149, 150, 153
- discussions, 126
- interviews, 18, 98
- job interviews, 138
- listening for key information, 159
- radio programs, 86
- ranking, 116
- restaurant orders, 46–47
- shopping, 110
- telephone calls, 58
- television programs, 6

PRONUNCIATION
- /b/ and /v/, /l/ and /r/ sounds, 87
- contractions of *be*, 6–7
- reduced form of *going to*, 98
- reduced form of *have*, 139
- reduced form of *what are you . . .*, 59
- reduced forms of *do you have . . .* and *would you like . . .*, 47
- rising and falling intonation, 110, 150
- rising intonation on lists, 30
- *should, shouldn't*, 126
- sounds of *-ed* endings, 70
- verbs that end in *-s*, 18

READING SKILLS, 10, 22, 34, 50, 62, 74, 90, 102, 114, 130, 142, 156

READINGS
- *Bugs as Food*, 50–51
- *The Cradle of the Inca Empire*, 74–75
- *Future Energy: Where Will We Get Our Energy?* 102–103
- *Humanity's Greatest Achievements*, 142–143
- *People from Around the World*, 10–11
- *The Secrets of Long Life*, 130–131
- *Silk–The Queen of Textiles*, 114–115
- *Smart Traveler*, 34–35
- TED Talks
  - *How to Buy Happiness*, 154–155
  - *The Interspecies Internet? An Idea in Progress*, 90–91
  - *My Mind-Shifting Everest Swim*, 62–63
  - *A Virtual Choir 2,000 Voices Strong*, 22–23

SPEAKING
- asking and answering questions, 5, 7, 17, 19, 31, 71, 99, 129, 132
- conversations, 5, 9, 17, 21, 29, 33, 45, 49, 57, 61, 69, 73, 85, 89, 97, 101, 109, 113, 125, 129, 137, 141, 149, 153
- comparing, 13, 59, 85, 109, 127
- describing, 7, 9, 16, 20, 21, 25, 41, 45, 49, 57, 64, 73, 76, 89, 113, 164–165
- discussing, 33, 53, 64, 65, 69, 71, 77, 78, 81, 90, 92, 97, 99, 102, 111, 114, 117, 118, 121, 127, 137, 141, 142, 144, 149, 154, 157, 160, 161
- exchanging information, 87

giving advice, 33, 40, 125, 126
giving opinions and reasons, 32
job interviews, 139
making predictions, 38, 78, 101
naming objects, 165
role-playing, 32, 37, 47, 65, 105, 116, 139
trip planning, 113, 151

TED TALKS
How to Buy Happiness, 158–161
The Interspecies Internet? An Idea in Progress, 118–121
My Mind-Shifting Everest Swim, 78–81
A Virtual Choir 2,000 Voices Strong, 38–41

TEST-TAKING SKILLS
categorizing, 60
checking off answers, 18, 47, 59, 70, 90, 98, 99, 104, 105, 111, 139, 140, 154, 158, 161
circling answers, 7, 8, 9, 16, 18, 25, 37, 61, 70, 74, 86, 117, 126, 150
completing charts, 19, 31, 41, 76, 86, 87, 92, 101, 111, 120, 127, 132, 145, 151, 159, 161
definitions, 148
fill in the blanks, 4, 5, 6, 9, 13, 18, 49, 57, 61, 65, 69, 71, 77, 78, 110, 117, 118, 145, 157
labeling pictures, 16, 38, 56, 60, 62, 72, 80, 84, 108, 136, 140
matching, 5, 30, 64, 68, 72, 93, 96, 97, 108, 118, 120, 128, 133, 137, 149, 150
multiple choice, 18, 22, 25, 70, 80, 86, 117, 129, 149, 150, 159, 160
ordering pictures, 28
ordering sentences, 157
ranking answers, 116, 144, 157
rewriting questions, 101
sentence completion, 9, 17, 20, 24, 28, 29, 32, 38, 45, 49, 64, 72, 73, 77, 80, 89, 97, 100, 101, 108, 109, 113, 124, 128, 137, 138, 142, 152, 153, 156, 160
sorting answers into columns, 8, 12, 25, 46, 48, 52, 60, 68, 84, 96, 104, 124
true or false, 10, 13, 25, 30, 34, 37, 40, 53, 62, 70, 77, 90, 93, 98, 112, 133, 142, 145
underlining answers, 74, 102, 108
unscrambling sentences, 9, 21, 68, 85, 149
writing requests and predictions, 85, 101
writing questions, 33, 101, 129

TOPICS
Achievements, 134–145
Communication, 82–93
Consequences, 146–157
Destinations, 66–77
Food, 42–53
Going Places, 26–37
Lifestyles, 122–133
Moving Forward, 94–105
People, 2–13
Sports, 54–65
Types of Clothing, 106–117
Work, Rest, and Play, 14–25

VIDEO JOURNAL
Beagle Patrol, 37
Cheese-Rolling Races, 65
Dangerous Dinner, 53
The Last of the Woman Divers, 13
Machu Picchu, 77
Monkey Business, 25
The Missing Snows of Kilimanjaro, 157
The Science of Stress, 133
Solar Cooking, 105
Spacewalk, 145
Traditional Silk Making, 117
Wild Animal Trackers, 93

VOCABULARY
achievements, 140
activities, 56, 58
animals, 152
chores, 136
clothing, 100, 108, 112
communication methods, 84
compound adjectives, 128
countries and nationalities, 4
daily routine, 16
descriptive adjectives, 8
diets, 48
emphatic adjectives, 72
festivals and celebrations, 20
food, 44, 48
habitats, 152
habits, 124
money, 32, 148
numbers, 30
occupations, 4
party words, 20
people, 4
planning, 96
senses, 88
sports, 56, 60
travel, 28, 32, 68
weather conditions, 100

WRITING
advice, 125
answering questions, 64, 116, 132
e-mails, 64, 156
job descriptions, 12
letters, 156
list-making, 13
make suggestions, 156
paragraphs, 24, 76, 104, 116, 132, 144
recipes, 52
statements about the future, 104
text messages, 92
travel blog, 71, 76
travel tips, 36
word webs, 14

CREDITS

ILLUSTRATION

4: (t) National Geographic Maps; **7:** (1 to 6) Nesbitt Graphics, Inc.; **8:** (lt and lb) Nesbitt Graphics, Inc.; **44:** (t) Keith Neely/IllustrationOnline.com; **45:** (b) Nesbitt Graphics, Inc.; **46:** (c) Nesbitt Graphics, Inc.; **48:** (t) Nesbitt Graphics, Inc.; **57:** (c) Rob Schuster; **88:** (t, tm, m, bm, b) Nesbitt Graphics, Inc.; **92:** (b) Rob Schuster; **108:** (t) Kenneth Batelman; **151:** (b) National Geographic Maps.

PHOTO

Cover Photo: Slow Images/Photographer's Choice/Getty Images

2–3: (c) Sigit Pamungkas/Reuters; **4:** (tl) Raul Touzon/National Geographic Creative, (bl) Robert George Young/Photographer's Choice/Getty Images, (tc) Robert Sisson/National Geographic Creative, (tlc) Damien Meyer/AFP/Getty Images, (trc) jochem wijnands/Horizons WWP/Alamy, (tr) Zhang Meng/Xinhua Press/Corbis, (rc) Daj/Getty Images, (br) Paul Bradbury/OJO Images/Getty Images; **6:** (tl) © iStockphoto.com/Peter Close, (tr) © iStockphoto.com/shotbydave, (blc) Simon Jarratt/Fancy/Corbis, (brc) © iStockphoto.com/yelo34; **7:** (tr) Roy Toft/National Geographic Creative; **8:** (tl) © iStockphoto.com/nicolesy, (tlc) Jupiterimages/Photos.com/Thinkstock, (trc) © iStockphoto.com/JLBarranco, (tr) © iStockphoto.com/diego_cervo, (bl) © iStockphoto.com/H-Gall, (blc) © iStockphoto.com/lmistock, (brc) © iStockphoto.com/Blue_Cutler, (br) © iStockphoto.com/epicurean; **9:** (tc) Michael Christopher Brown/National Geographic Creative; **10–11:** (rc) Kevin Fleming/National Geographic Creative; **11:** (tr) Priscilla Gragg/Blend Images/Alamy, (tc) William Albert Allard/National Geographic Image Collection; **12:** (tc) Alex Treadway/National Geographic Creative, (lc) Steve Raymer/National Geographic Creative, (bl) Simon Jarratt/Ivy/Corbis; **13:** (tc) Vincent Prevost/Hemis/Terra/Corbis, (rc) He Lulu Xinhua News Agency/Newscom; **14–15:** (c) Stringer/Reuters; **16:** (tl) © iStockphoto.com/Juanmonino, (tc) © iStockphoto.com/Justin Horrocks, (tr) Bob Scott/Photodisc/Thinkstock, (lc) Keith Brofsky/Photodisc/Thinkstock, (c) Fuse/Getty Images, (rc) Andrea Chu/Photodisc/Thinkstock, (lc) © iStockphoto.com/BartekSzewczyk, (c) © iStockphoto.com/avdeev007, (rc) © Monkey Business Images/Shutterstock.com, (bl) Fuse/Thinkstock, (bc) © iStockphoto.com/Rich Legg, (br) © iStockphoto.com/DIGIcal; **17:** (br) Joe Raedle/Getty Images; **18:** (tc) Adam Crowley/Blend Images/Getty Images; **20:** (tc) India Picture/Collage/Corbis, (lc) Jupiterimages/Photos.com/Thinkstock, (bl) Scott Stulberg/Comet/Corbis; **22:** (l) Mike Pont/Getty Images Entertainment/Getty Images, (c) Roberto Serra - Iguana Press/Getty Images Entertainment/Getty Images, (r) C Brandon/Redferns/Redferns/Getty Images; **23:** (c) James Duncan Davidson/TED, (inset) Gallo Images/Getty Images News/Getty Images; **24:** (t) Chad Springer/Corbis, (bl, bc, br) TED; **25:** (tc) Narong Sangnak/epa/Corbis Wire/Corbis; **26–27:** (c) Kani Polat/500px Prime; **28:** (tl) © iStockphoto.com/leezsnow, (tc) © iStockphoto.com/Neustockimages, (tr) © Galyna Andrushko/Shutterstock.com, (lc) © James Steidl/Shutterstock.com, (c) Hemera Technologies/Photos.com/Thinkstock, (rc) Bruno Domingos/Reuters/Corbis, (bl) Digital Vision/Getty Images, (bc) TongRo Images/Harry Choi/Alamy, (br) Timur Kulgarin/Shutterstock.com, (bl) Fuse/Thinkstock; **29:** (br) Skip Brown/National Geographic Creative; **30:** (tc) Bill Bachmann/Science Source; **31:** (tc) Mike Theiss/National Geographic Creative; **32:** (tl) © emilie zhang/Shutterstock.com, (tlc) AP Images/Rebecca D'Angelo, (lc) Imagedoc/Alamy, (blc) © Oleksiy Mark/Shutterstock.com, (bl) Martin Shields/Alamy, (c) Andrew Woodley/Alamy, (rc) Alan Myers/Alamy; **33:** (br) Andria Patino/Encyclopedia/Corbis; **34–35:** (rc) Jimmy Chim/National Geographic Creative; **36:** (tc) Pola Damonte/Moment Open/Getty Images; **37:** (tc) Lauralea Lasher/National Geographic Creative, (rc) european pressphoto agency b.v./Alamy; **38:** (1) © Jonathan Lewis/Shutterstock.com, (2) © criben/Shutterstock.com, (3) © Aschindl/Shutterstock.com, (4) © muzsy/Shutterstock.com; **39:** (t) James Duncan Davidson/TED, (bl, br, t) TED; **40:** (t) TED; **41:** (t) Christian Vorhofer/imagebroker/Corbis; **42:** (c) Lucy Vaserfirer/500px Prime; **45:** (cl) © iStockphoto.com/PaulCowan, (b) © iStockphoto.com/Andrea Skjold, (cr) © iStockphoto.com/1 design; **46:** (t) Jonathan Kingston/National Geographic Creative; **47:** (r) Chris Howes/Wild Places Photography/Alamy; **48:** (1) © Dionisvera/Shutterstock.com, (2) © g215/Shutterstock.com, (3) © zcw/Shutterstock.com, (4) © Gordo25/Shutterstock.com, (5) © iStockphoto.com/jaker5000, (6) © Elena Schweitzer/Shutterstock.com, (7) © iStockphoto.com/alex-mit, (8) © GVictoria/Shutterstock.com; **50:** (l) Kevin Foy/Alamy, (inset) f4foto/Alamy; **51:** (tr) Dan Kitwood/Getty Images News/Getty Images; **52:** (t) Rolf Nussbaumer/imagebroker/Canopy/Corbis; **53:** (t) Brian J. Skerry/National Geographic Creative, (1) © Alexius Sutandio/Shutterstock.com, (2) lilithlita/iStock/360/Getty Images, (3) Ben Horton/National Geographic Creative, (4) Ben Horton/National Geographic Creative; **54:** (c) Courtesy Tim Kemple; **56:** (1) Lear Miller Photo/Image Source/Alamy, (2) © iStockphoto.com/isitsharp, (3) Francesco Tremolada/SOPA RF/Ramble/Corbis, (4) Tim McGuire/Comet/Corbis, (5) © iStockphoto.com/Mari, (6) JGI/Jamie Grill/Blend Images/Getty Images, (7) © oliveromg/Shutterstock.com; **57:** (r) Jill Schneider/National Geographic Creative; **58:** (tl) © Monkey Business Images/Shutterstock.com, (tc) © Bull's-Eye Arts/Shutterstock.com, (tr) © Diego Cervo/Shutterstock.com, (bl) © Aspen Photo/Shutterstock.com, (bc) Jupiterimages/Stockbyte/Thinkstock, (br) © iStockphoto.com/buckarooh; **59:** (t) Michael Hanson/National Geographic Creative; **60:** (tl) © Mayskyphoto/Shutterstock.com, (tr) Koki Nagahama/Getty Images Sport/Getty Images, (bl) © Sergey_Peterman/Shutterstock.com, (br) © Nikolpetr/Shutterstock.com; **61:** (r) Keith Ladzinski/alex-honnold-MR.pdf/alex-lowthe/Aurora/Passage/Corbis; **62:** (tl, tr, bl, br) TED; **63:** (t) Darren Staples/Reuters, (c) AP Images/MTI/Peter Komka, 63 (c) James Duncan Davis, 63 (inset) © 7382489561/Shutterstock.com, (b) Ryan Pierse/Getty Images Sport/Getty Images; **64:** (t) © iStockphoto.com/DanielPrudek; **66:** (c) Jim Richardson/National Geographic Creative; **68:** (1) © Konstantin Sutyagin /Shutterstock.com, (2) © iStockphoto.com/Tempura, (3) © iStockphoto.com/ImagesbyTrista, (4) Richard Wong/Alamy, (5) © iStockphoto.com/1001nights, (6) © iStockphoto.com/RiverNorthPhotography, (7) Max Alexander/Dorling Kindersley/Getty Images; **69:** (r) Alison Wright/National Geographic Creative; **70:** (l) Joseph C. Justice Jr/Getty Images; **71:** (t) Beverly Joubert/National Geographic Creative, (b) Dmitry Rukhlenko/Travel Photos/Alamy; **72:** (tl) Jamie Grill/JGI/Blend Images/Alamy, (tr) Michael Hanson/National Geographic Creative; **73:** (r) Tim Laman/

National Geographic Creative; **74:** (b) Hiram Bingham/National Geographic Creative; **75:** (tr) Hiram Bingham/National Geographic Creative, (c) Micheal Melford/National Geographic Creative; **76:** (t) © WitR/Shutterstock.com; **77:** (t) Johnny's photography/Moment/Getty Images; **78:** (tl) FRANS LANTING/National Geographic Creative, (tr) BORGE OUSLAND/National Geographic Creative, (bl) © 7382489561/Shutterstock.com, (br) MIKE THEISS/National Geographic Creative; **79:** (t) James Duncan Davidson/TED, (bl) MIKE THEISS/National Geographic Creative, (bc, br) TED; **81:** (t) RICHARD OLSENIUS /National Geographic Creative, (tl) RALPH LEE HOPKINS/National Geographic Creative, (tr) MIKE THEISS/National Geographic Creative, (bl) SKIP BROWN/National Geographic Creative, (br) PETE MCBRIDE/National Geographic Creative; **82:** (c) Petra Warner and Wolf Park; **84:** (1) © PaulPaladin/Shutterstock.com, (2) © iStockphoto.com/JaminWell, (3) © Steven Frame/Shutterstock.com, (4) Wavebreakmedia Ltd/Thinkstock, (5) Ingram Publishing/Thinkstock, (6) © Forest Badger/Shutterstock.com, (7) © Feng Yu/Shutterstock.com, (8) © bloomua/Shutterstock.com; **86:** (t) Nicole Duplaix/National Geographic Creative, (l) © StepStock/Shutterstock.com; **88:** (1) © iStockphoto.com/ALEAIMAGE, (2) © Edyta Pawlowska/Shutterstock.com, (3) © iStockphoto.com/cveltri, (4) © iStockphoto.com/jallfree, (5) © iStockphoto.com/Atlanta-Mike, (6) Fuse/Thinkstock, (7) © Monkey Business Images/Shutterstock.com, (8) Michael Blann/Digital Vision/Thinkstock; **89:** (t) David Coleman/Alamy; **91:** (c) James Duncan Davidson/TED; (inset) RALPH LEE HOPKINS/National Geographic Creative; **92:** (t) DAVID DOUBILET/National Geographic Creative; **93:** (t) RALPH LEE HOPKINS/National Geographic Creative; **94:** (c) XPACIFICA/National Geographic Creative; **96:** (1) © iStockphoto.com/Danila Krylov, (2) Top Photo Group/Thinkstock, (3) © iStockphoto.com/asiseeit/Steve Debenport, (4) © iStockphoto.com/Digitalskillet, (5) © iStockphoto.com/joxxxxjo, (6) Andrew Olney/Photodisc/Thinkstock, (7) © iStockphoto.com/YinYang, (8) Fuse/Thinkstock; **97:** (b) cotesebastien/iStock/360/Getty Images; **98:** (l) © MrKornFlakes/Shutterstock.com; **99:** (t) Bill Ross/Comet/Corbis; **100:** (1) © Alexander Shalamov/Shutterstock.com, (2) © Jozsef Szasz-Fabian/Shutterstock.com, (3) © iStockphoto.com/Floortje, (4) © Nikolay Postnikov/Shutterstock.com, (5) © iStockphoto.com/Oktay Ortakcioglu, 100 (6) © iStockphoto.com/evemilla, (7) © studioVin/Shutterstock.com, (8) © sunabesyou/Shutterstock.com; **101:** (b) Michael Melford/National Geographic Creative; **102:** (c) MICHAEL MELFORD/National Geographic Creative; **104:** (t) Detlev van Ravenswaay/Picture Press/Getty Images; **105:** (t) Orjan F. Ellingvag/Dagens Naringsliv/Corbis News Premium/Corbis, (1) © vovan/Shutterstock.com, (2) © Alex Kuzovlev/Shutterstock.com, (3) © iStockphoto.com/WendellandCarolyn, (4) © iStockphoto.com/visdia, (5) Medford Taylor/National Geographic Creative; **106:** (c) Amy Toensing; **110:** (t) Cheryl Chan/Moment Open/Getty Images; **112:** (l) © iStockphoto.com/Jitalia17, (cl) © iStockphoto.com/AlexKalina, (c) © sagir/Shutterstock.com, (cr) © iStockphoto.com/itsjustluck, (r) Photos.com/360/Getty Images; **114:** (l) Luis Marden/National Geographic Creative, (r) oytun karadayi/E+/Getty Images; **115:** (c) Jason Edwards/National Geographic Creative; **116:** (t) Keren Su/Terra/Corbis; **117:** (t) Amy White & Al Petteway /National Geographic Creative; **119:** (t) James Duncan Davidson/TED, (hl, bc, br) TED; **120:** (t) AFP/Stringer/Getty Images; **122:** (c) DAVID DOUBILET/National Geographic Creative; **124:** (1) Jamie Grill/The Image Bank/Getty Images, (2) © iStockphoto.com/Silvrshootr, (3) © iStockphoto.com/enad, (4) © Lukasz Fus/Shutterstoc.com, (5) © iStockphoto.com/DanielBendjy, (6) © iStockphoto.com/digitalskillet, (7) © alicedaniel/Shutterstock.com, (8) ArkReligion.com/Art Directors & TRIP/Alamy, (9) © iStockphoto.com/bloodstone; **126:** (1) 101dalmatians/E+/Getty Images, (2) © iStockphoto.com/Brendan McIlhargey , (3) ©iStockphoto.com/lostinbids/jo unruh; **127:** (t) Brigitte Sporrer/Cultura/Getty Images; **128:** (t) Image Source/Getty Images; **129:** (r) Andersen Ross/Digital Vision/Getty Images; **131:** (r) Roberto Defraia - RobMcfrey/Moment/Getty Images, (inset) David McLain/National Geographic Image Collection; **132:** (t) Thomas Barwick/Iconica/Getty Images; **133:** Atlantide Phototravel/Corbis; **134:** (c) John Burcham/National Geographic Creative; **136:** (1) © Monkey Business Images/Shutterstock.com, (2) © katja kodba/Shutterstock.com, (3) © Sonya etchison/Shutterstock.com, (4) © Anne Kitzman/Shutterstock.com, (5) © iStockphoto.com/jwohlfeil, (6) © iStockphoto.com/Tomaz Levstek, (7) © iStockphoto.com/Klubovy, (8) Andrey Kekyalyaynen/Alamy; **137:** (b) Willie B. Thomas/E+/Getty Images; **138:** (t) IRA Block/National Geographic Creative; **139:** (b) Medford Taylor/National Geographic Creative; **140:** (1) © iStockphoto.com/GlobalStock, (2) Fang Chun Che/Dreamstime.com, (3) © Koh sze kiat /Shutterstock.com, (4) © iStockphoto.com/Gene Chutka, (5) Eric Audras/PhotoAlto/Alamy, (6) wavebreakmedia Ltd/Thinkstock; **141:** (r) © Songquan Deng/Shutterstock.com; **142:** (inset) RICHARD NOWITZ/National Geographic Creative; **143:** (full) Kenneth Garrett/National Geographic Creative; **144:** (t) NASA/National Geographic Creative, (t) Corbis; **145:** (t) NASA/ESA/National Geographic Creative; **146:** (c) Joshua Holko www.jholko.com; **148:** (tl) Jim Richardson/National Geographic Creative, (c) Eric Audras/PhotoAlto/Alamy; **150:** (t) Towfiqu Photography/Moment/Getty Images; **151:** (tr) Marc Moritsch/National Geographic Creative; **152:** (1) © iStockphoto.com/Angel Herrero de Frutos, (2) © kavram/Shutterstock.com, (3, 4) FRANS LANTING/National Geographic Creative, (5) © marcoap1974/Shutterstock.com, (6) © iStockphoto.com/Ammit, (7) Richard Nowitz/National Geographic Creative, (8) © ShaneGross/Shutterstock.com, (9) Michael S. Quinton/National Geographic Creative, (10) © HonzaHruby/Shutterstock.com; **153:** (tr) FRANS LANTING/National Geographic Creative; **155:** (t) Justin Ide/TED, (inset) Pascal Deloche/Godong/Corbis; **156:** (t) Jeremy Woodhouse/Blend Images/Corbis; **157:** (t) Michele Burgess/Photolibrary/Getty Images; **159:** (t) Justin Ide/TED , (l, rt, rc, rb) TED; **160:** (t) Jason Edwards/National Geographic Creative.

Workbook

WORLD ENGLISH 1

SECOND EDITION

Real People • Real Places • Real Language

Kristin L. Johannsen, Author
Rob Jenkins, Series Editor

Australia • Brazil • Japan • Korea • Mexico • Singapore • Spain • United Kingdom • United States

World English Level 1 Workbook
Real People, Real Places, Real Language
Kristin L. Johannsen, Author
Rob Jenkins, Series Editor

Publisher: Sherrise Roehr

Executive Editor: Sarah Kenney

Senior Development Editor: Margarita Matte

Development Editor: Brenden Layte

Assistant Editor: Alison Bruno

Editorial Assistant: Patricia Giunta

Media Researcher: Leila Hishmeh

Senior Technology Product Manager: Scott Rule

Director of Global Marketing: Ian Martin

Senior Product Marketing Manager:
    Caitlin Thomas

Senior Director of ELT Production:
    Michael Burggren

Production Manager: Daisy Sosa

Content Project Manager: Andrea Bobotas

Senior Print Buyer: Mary Beth Hennebury

Cover Designer: Aaron Opie

Art Director: Scott Baker

Creative Director: Chris Roy

Cover Image: Slow Images/Getty Images

Compositor: MPS Limited

Copyright © 2015, 2010 National Geographic Learning, a part of Cengage Learning

ALL RIGHTS RESERVED. No part of this work covered by the copyright herein may be reproduced, transmitted, stored or used in any form or by any means graphic, electronic, or mechanical, including but not limited to photocopying, recording, scanning, digitizing, taping, Web distribution, information networks, or information storage and retrieval systems, except as permitted under Section 107 or 108 of the 1976 United States Copyright Act, without the prior written permission of the publisher.

> For product information and technology assistance, contact us at
> **Cengage Learning Customer & Sales Support, 1-800-354-9706**
> For permission to use material from this text or product,
> submit all requests online at **cengage.com/permissions**
> Further permissions questions can be emailed to
> **permissionrequest@cengage.com**

World English Intro Workbook ISBN: 978-1-285-84843-3

National Geographic Learning
20 Channel Center Street
Boston, MA 02210
USA

Cengage Learning is a leading provider of customized learning solutions with office locations around the globe, including Singapore, the United Kingdom, Austrailia, Mexico, Brazil, and Japan.

Cengage Learning products are represented in Canada by Nelson Education, Ltd.

Visit National Geographic Learning online at ngl.cengage.com

Visit our corporate website at www.cengage.com

Printed in the United States of America
1 2 3 4 5 6 7 8 9 10   16 15 14

CONTENTS

Scope and Sequence iv
Credits viii
Unit 1 People 9
Unit 2 Work, Rest, And Play 15
Unit 3 Going Places 21
Unit 4 Food 27
Unit 5 Sports 33
Unit 6 Destinations 39

STUDENT BOOK SCOPE AND SEQUENCE

Split A	Unit Goals	Grammar	Vocabulary
UNIT 1 People Page 2	• Meet people • Ask for and give personal information • Describe different occupations • Describe positive and negative parts of occupations	Review of Present tense: *Be* *Be* + adjective (+ noun) Possessive adjectives	Occupations Countries Nationalities Descriptive adjectives
UNIT 2 Work, Rest, and Play Page 14	• Talk about a typical day • Talk about free time • Describe a special celebration or festival • Describe daily life in different communities	Review: Simple present tense Prepositions of time Adverbs of frequency	Daily activities Party words Celebrations and festivals
UNIT 3 Going Places Page 26	• Identify possessions • Ask for and give personal travel information • Give travel advice • Share special travel tips with others	Possession Imperatives and *should* for advice	Travel preparations and stages Ordinal numbers Travel documents and money

TEDTALKS Video Page 38 Eric Whitacre: A Virtual Choir 2,000 Voices Strong

UNIT 4 Food Page 42	• Give a recipe • Order a meal • Talk about diets • Discuss unusual foods	Count and non-count nouns: *some* and *any* *How much* and *How many* with quantifiers: *lots of, a few, a little*	Food Food groups Diets
UNIT 5 Sports Page 54	• Describe activities happening now • Compare everyday and present-time activities • Talk about favorite sports • Discuss adventures	Present continuous tense Stative verbs	Doing sports Present-time activities Team sports and individual sports
UNIT 6 Destinations Page 66	• Discuss past vacations • Exchange information about vacations • Use *was/were* to describe a personal experience • Describe a discovery from the past	Simple past tense Simple past tense of *to be*	Travel activities Emphatic adjectives

TEDTALKS Video Page 78 Lewis Pugh: My Mind-Shifting Everest Swim

Listening	Speaking and Pronunciation	Reading	Writing	Video Journal
Focused listening: Personal introductions	Asking for and giving personal information Contractions of *be*: –'m, –'re, –'s	**National Geographic:** "People from Around the World"	Writing about people's occupations and nationalities	**National Geographic:** "The Last of The Woman Divers"
Focused listening: A radio celebrity interview	Talking about daily schedules and free time Verbs that end in *–s*	**TED**TALKS "Eric Whitacre: A Virtual Choir 2,000 Voices Strong"	Writing a descriptive paragraph about daily routines Writing Strategy: Word web	**National Geographic:** "Monkey Business"
General listening: Conversations at travel destinations	Giving personal information for travel forms Rising intonation on lists	**National Geographic:** "Smart Traveler"	Writing travel tips	**National Geographic:** "Beagle Patrol"
General and focused listening: Ordering a meal in a restaurant	Role-play: Purchasing food at a supermarket Reduced forms: *Do you have . . .* and *Would you like . . .*	**National Geographic:** "Bugs as Food"	Writing a recipe	**National Geographic:** "Dangerous Dinner"
General and focused listening: Everyday activities vs. today's activities	Talking about what people are doing now Discussing favorite sports Reduced form: *What are you . . .*	**TED**TALKS "Lewis Pugh: My Mind-Shifting Everest Swim"	Writing an e-mail	**National Geographic:** "Cheese-Rolling Races"
General listening: A vacation	Comparing vacations Describing personal experiences Sounds of *–ed* endings	**National Geographic:** "The Cradle of the Inca Empire"	Writing a travel blog	**National Geographic:** "Machu Picchu"

Split B	Unit Goals	Grammar	Vocabulary
UNIT 7 Communication Page 82	• Talk about personal communication • Exchange contact information • Describe characteristics and qualities • Compare different types of communication	Verbs with direct and indirect objects Irregular past tense Sensory verbs	Communication Electronics The senses
UNIT 8 Moving Forward Page 94	• Talk about plans • Discuss long- and short-term plans • Make weather predictions • Discuss the future	Future tense: *be going to* *Will* for predictions and immediate decisions	Short- and long-term plans Weather conditions Weather-specific clothing
UNIT 9 Types of Clothing Page 106	• Make comparisons • Explain preferences • Talk about clothing materials • Evaluate quality and value	Comparatives Superlatives	Clothing Descriptive adjectives Clothing materials

TEDTALKS Video Page 118 Diana Reiss: Peter Gabriel, Neil Gershenfeld, Vint Cerf: The Interspecies Internet? An Idea in Progress

UNIT 10 Lifestyles Page 122	• Give advice on healthy habits • Compare lifestyles • Ask about lifestyles • Evaluate your lifestyle	Modals (*could, ought to, should, must*); *have to* Questions with *how*	Healthy and unhealthy habits Compound adjectives
UNIT 11 Achievements Page 134	• Talk about today's chores • Interview for a job • Talk about personal accomplishments • Discuss humanity's greatest achievements	Present perfect tense Present perfect tense vs. simple past tense	Chores Personal accomplishments
UNIT 12 Consequences Page 146	• Talk about managing your money • Make choices on how to spend your money • Talk about cause and effect • Evaluate money and happiness	Real conditionals (also called the first conditional)	Personal finance Animals Animal habitats

TEDTALKS Video Page 158 Michael Norton: How to Buy Happiness

Listening	Speaking and Pronunciation	Reading	Writing	Video Journal
Focused listening: A radio call-in program	Asking for contact information Describing sights, sounds and other sensations The /b/ and /v/, /l/ and /r/ sounds	**TED**TALKS "Diana Reiss, Peter Gabriel, Neil Gershenfeld, Vint Cerf: The Interspecies Internet? An Idea in Progress"	Writing a text message Make a list	**National Geographic:** "Wild Animal Trackers"
General listening: A talk show	Talking about weekend plans Discussing the weather Reduced form of *going to*	**National Geographic:** "Future Energy"	Writing statements about the future	**National Geographic:** "Solar Cooking"
Focused listening: Shoe shopping	Talking about clothes Shopping—at the store and online Rising and falling intonation	**National Geographic:** "Silk—the Queen of Textiles"	Writing about buying clothes	**National Geographic:** "How Your T-Shirt Can Make a Difference"
General listening: Personal lifestyles	Discussing healthy and unhealthy habits Asking and telling about lifestyles *Should, shouldn't*	**National Geographic:** "The Secrets of Long Life"	Writing a paragraph about personal lifestyle	**National Geographic:** "The Science of Stress"
Listening for general understanding and specific details: A job interview	Interviewing for a job Catching up with a friend Reduced form of *have*	**National Geographic:** "Humanity's Greatest Achievements"	Writing about achievements	**National Geographic:** "Spacewalk"
Listening for specific details: At a travel agency Listening for key information	Making decisions about spending money Talking about important environmental issues Intonation, sentence stress	**TED**TALKS "Michael Norton: How to Buy Happiness"	Write about cause and effect Writing Strategy: Make suggestions	**National Geographic:** "The Missing Snows of Kilimanjaro"

CREDITS

ILLUSTRATION:
10: Ted Hammond/IllustrationsOnline.com; **15:** Mark Collins/IllustrationsOnline.com; **22:** Jim Atherton; **27:** Ted Hammond/IllustrationsOnline.com; **31, 53:** Jim Atherton; **60:** Nesbitt Graphics, Inc.; **75:** Keith Neely/IllustrationsOnline.com; **78:** Nesbitt Graphics, Inc.

PHOTO
Cover Photo: Slow Images/Photographer's Choice/Getty Images

9: (1) Evgenia Pashkova/iStock/Thinkstock; (2) © Warren Goldswain / Shutterstock.com; (3) Hill Street Studios/Blend Images/Getty Images; (4) © michaeljung/Shutterstock.com; (5) © iStockphoto.com/RobMattingley; (6) ColorBlind Images/Blend Images/Thinkstock; (7) © ra2studio/Shutterstock.com; (8) © Vasiliy Koval/Shutterstock.com; (bottom) © leelook/Shutterstock.com; **11:** (top) © iStockphoto.com/JohnnyGreig; (middle) © lzf/Shutterstock.com; (bottom) © g-stockstudio/Shutterstock.com; **12:** (top) George F. Mobley/National Geographic Creative; (top middle) © Stephen Coburn/Shutterstock.com; (bottom middle) Wilfried Krecichwost/The Image Bank/Getty Images; (bottom) Photo and Co/The Image Bank/Getty Images; **13:** (top) Jupiterimages/Stockbyte/Thinkstock; (bottom) © michaeljung/Shutterstock.com; **15:** (top) © IVY PHOTOS/Shutterstock.com; **16:** © StockLite/Shutterstock.com; **17:** (1) © Sergei Bachlakov/Shutterstock.com; (2) David Sacks/Photodisc/Getty Images; (3) © iStockphoto.com/Creativel/Oksana Struk; (4) © iStockphoto.com/emreogan; (5) © solarseven/Shutterstock.com; (6) © Anton Albert/Shutterstock.com; **18:** (top) © Gertjan Hooijer/Shutterstock.com; (middle) Roger Parkes/Alamy; (bottom) Blue Jean Images/Getty Images; **19:** Jason Edwards/National Geographic Creative; **21:** (top) © Jacqui Martin/Shutterstock.com; (1) © AVAVA/Shutterstock.com; (2) © Stephen Coburn/Shutterstock.com; (3) © iStockphoto.com/TriggerPhoto; (4) Emmanuel Faure/Taxi/Getty Images; (5) Ryan McVay/Photodisc/Thinkstock; (6) © Blend Images/Shutterstock.com; **23:** (top) © iStockphoto.com/jasantiso; (top middle) © Brian A Jackson/Shutterstock.com; (middle) © iStockphoto.com/Chalabala; (bottom middle) © iStockphoto.com/BVDC; (bottom) © iStockphoto.com/Creativeye99; **24:** (top) Fuse/Thinkstock; (bottom) Stockbyte/Thinkstock; **28:** Hill Street Studios/Blend Images/Thinkstock; **29:** (1) © infografick/Shutterstock.com; (2) © Svetlana Foote/Shutterstock.com; (3) © Osvaldru/Shutterstock.com; (4) © shutterdandan/Shutterstock.com; (5) © Aaron Amat/Shutterstock.com; (6) © Oliver Hoffmann/Shutterstock.com; (7) © MSPhotographic/Shutterstock.com; (8) © Silvia Bogdanski/Shutterstock.com; (right top) © Tony Wear/Shutterstock.com; (Right bottom) © Creatista/Shutterstock.com; **30:** (top) Amanda Heywood/Food And Drink Photos/AGE Fotostock; (top middle) © iStockphoto.com/Lehner Lehner; (middle) © iStockphoto.com/iMychkoAlezander; (bottom) Ros Drinkwater/Alamy; **33:** (1) © iStockphoto.com/Frantysek; (2) Zoonar RF/Thinkstock; (3) © Vixit/Shutterstock.com; (4) © iStockphoto.com/RyanJLane; (5) © 2xSamara.com/Shutterstock.com; (6) © iStockphoto.com/Alexey2075; **34:** (1) © Paul Clarke/Shutterstock.com; (2) © Goran Bogicevic/Shutterstock.com; (3) © iStockphoto.com/Joe_Potato; (4) © iStockphoto.com/bowdenimages; (5) © iStockphoto.com/Rich Legg; (6) ©Ta Khum/Shutterstock.com; **35:** (1) © Denis Pepin/Shutterstock.com; (2) © Andresr/Shutterstock.com; (3) © iStockphoto.com/ftwitty; (4) © Mike Flippo/Shutterstock.com; (5) © Prod-akszyn/Shutterstock.com; (6) © versh/Shutterstock.com; (7) © iStockphoto.com/leomedia; (8) © iStockphoto.com/hero30; **36:** (right top) MikeThesis/National Geographic Creative; (right top middle) Cavan Images/Getty Images; (Right middle) RICHARD NOWITZ/National Geographic Creative; (right bottom) (middle) © iStockphoto.com/Nikada; (right bottom) © iStockphoto.com/RBFried; (left bottom) © iStockphoto.com/ImagineGolf; (bottom middle) © iStockphoto.com/bonnie jacobs; **39:** (top) © Maceofoto/Shutterstock.com; (bottom) © iStockphoto.com/IlexImage; **40:** (top) © iStockphoto.com/Mlenny; (top middle) RICHARD NOWITZ/National Geographic Creative; (bottom middle) © iStockphoto.com/anouchka/Anna Bryukhanova; (bottom) © iStockphoto.com/compassandcamera; **41:** (Left) © iStockphoto.com/fotostok_pdv; (middle) © iStockphoto.com/luoman; (Right) Monkey Business Images/Dreamstime.com; **42:** © iStockphoto.com/cdwheatley; **43:** (top) © iStockphoto.com/Dhuss; (bottom) © Renata Sedmakova/Shutterstock.com; **45:** (1) © racorn/Shutterstock.com; (2) © bloomua/Shutterstock.com; (3) © chaoss/Shutterstock.com; (4) © Medioimages/Photodisc/Thinkstock; (5) Thomas Lohnes/Stringer/Getty Images; News/Getty Images; (6) © BigLike Images/Shutterstock.com; **47:** (1) Colorburst/Dreamstime.com; (2) © Darren Baker/Shutterstock.com; (3) © Hurst Photo/Shutterstock.com; (4) © iStockphoto.com/themacx; (5) © iStockphoto.com/Maximastudio; **48:** (top) © iStockphoto.com/Alexandr Pakhnyushchyy; (bottom left) © Ewan Chesser/Shutterstock.com; (bottom right) © iStockphoto.com/Spydr; **49:** (top) © iStockphoto.com/irvingnsaperstein; (middle) © Labrador Photo Video/Shutterstock.com; (bottom) © iStockphoto.com/ArtMarie; **51:** (top) © Ksenia Ragozina/Shutterstock.com; (bottom left) © iStockphoto.com/Jennifer Sharp; (bottom right) © iStockphoto.com/ktmoffitt; **52:** © iStockphoto.com/Chris Schmidt; **54:** (left top) © iStockphoto.com/btrenkel; (left middle) © iStockphoto.com/IS_ImageSource; (left right) © iStockphoto.com/monkeybusinessimages; (Right) © iStockphoto.com/Blend_Images; **55:** (top) Colin Gray/Photonica/Getty Images; (middle) © Monkey Business Images/Shutterstock.com; (Right) Joe Penney/Reuters; **57:** (1) © iStockphoto.com/Floortje; (2) © Gulei Ivan/Shutterstock.com; (3) © indigolotos/Shutterstock.com; (4) © terekhov igor/Shutterstock.com; (5) © iStockphoto.com/AleksandrL; (6) Helene Rogers/Art Directors & TRIP/Alamy; (7) © Photobac/Shutterstock.com; (8) © iStockphoto.com/Antagain; (9) © iStockphoto.com/Gary Alvis; (10) © iStockphoto.com/WEKWEK; (11) © Marko Poplasen/Shutterstock.com; (12) © Karkas/Shutterstock.com; **58:** moodboard/Alamy; **59:** (1) © Sean Pavone/Shutterstock.com; (2) © iStockphoto.com/nano; (3) © Sandra Cunningham/Shutterstock.com; (4) © iStockphoto.com/nazdravie/Paul Velgos; (5) © Paul Cowan/Shutterstock.com; **63:** © B. and E. Dudzinscy/Shutterstock.com; **64:** (top) © Mast3r/Shutterstock.com; (middle) © iStockphoto.com/Ken Tannenbaum; (bottom) © Blend Images/Shutterstock.com; **65:** © iStockphoto.com/alptraum; **66:** (Left) © Galina Barskaya/Shutterstock.com; (middle) © Diego Cervo/Shutterstock.com; (bottom right) © iStockphoto.com/4774344sean; (right middle) © iStockphoto.com/OJO_Images; (top right) Eric Farrelly/Alamy; **70:** (top) © iStockphoto.com/nycshooter/Michael Krinke; (bottom) © Olexiy Bayev/Shutterstock.com; **71:** Suprijono Suharjoto/Dreamstime.com; **72:** Karwai Tang/Getty Images; Entertainment/Getty Images; **73:** (top) Jim Campbell, Aero-News Network/NASA; (bottom) Xavier Arnau/E+/Getty Images; **76:** (top) © Uros Jonic/Shutterstock.com; **77:** (1) © Seleznev Oleg/Shutterstock.com; (2) © Zacarias Pereira da Mata/Shutterstock.com; (3) © Oliver Hoffmann /Shutterstock.com; (4) Frank/Helen Screider/National Geographic Creative; (5) © l i g h t p o e t/Shutterstock.com; **78:** (top) Roy Hsu/Photographer's Choice/Getty Images; (middle) © Vilainecrevette / Shutterstock.com; (bottom) © Piotr Sikora/Shutterstock.com; **79:** (top) © Pichugin Dmitry/Shutterstock.com; (middle) © Paul Clarke/Shutterstock.com; (bottom) © iStockphoto.com/Steve Rosset.

PEOPLE

UNIT 1

Lesson A GRAMMAR AND VOCABULARY

A Unscramble the job titles. Complete the sentences.

1. (hpootragephr) He's a __photographer__.
2. (nolitpcaii) She's a _____.
3. (cnadre) He's a _____.
4. (fche) She's a _____.
5. (icelop fofcire) She's a _____.
6. (tolpi) He's a _____.
7. (lervta getna) He's a _____.
8. (anjtiulros) She's a _____.

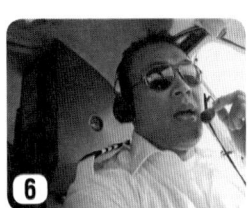

B Write the nationality.

1. France __French__
2. Jordan _____
3. Ireland _____
4. Japan _____
5. Australia _____
6. Peru _____
7. Mexico _____
8. Your nationality: _____

C Read the conversations. Write the pronouns and the correct form of *be*.

Cristina: Where (1) __are you__ from, Mike?

Mike: (2) _____ from Australia.

Cristina: So, (3) _____ Australian. Sounds cool. (4) _____ from Sydney?

Mike: Yes, I am. And you, Cristina? (5) _____ Mexican?

Cristina: No, (6) _____. (7) _____ Brazilian.

Mike: Wow! Brazil. I'd love to go to Brazil. Which city (8) _____ from?

Cristina: (9) _____ from Rio de Janeiro. (10) _____ a cool city!

People 9

Lesson B GRAMMAR AND VOCABULARY

A *What's My Name?* is a TV show. Read the information below and complete the sentences.

Name: Anita Age: 23 Nationality: Mexican City: Puebla Job: travel agent	Name: Isabel Age: 25 Nationality: Chilean City: Santiago Job: travel agent	Name: Carmen Age: 25 Nationality: Mexican City: Mexico City Job: dancer

Contestant: (1) __Are you__ a travel agent?

Woman #1: (2) _____, I am.

Contestant: And (3) _____ Chilean?

Woman #1: No, (4) _____.

Contestant: Hmm. So, you're Mexican.

Woman #1: Yes, (5) _____.

Contestant: Are you 23 (6) _____?

Woman #1: Yes!

Contestant: Is (7) _____ Anita?

Woman #1: Yes! You're right!

Contestant: Are you Mexican?

Woman #2: Yes, (8) _____.

Contestant: (9) _____ 25 years old?

Woman #2: Yes.

Contestant: Are you a travel agent?

Woman #2: No, (10) _____.

Contestant: So, (11) _____ a dancer.

Woman #2: Yes. You're right.

Contestant: Is your name Carmen?

Woman #2: Yes, (12) _____!

B Write the contractions.

1. I am __I'm__
2. she is _____
3. it is _____
4. you are _____
5. is not _____
6. we are _____

PEOPLE
UNIT 1

Lesson C GRAMMAR AND VOCABULARY

A Match the opposites.

1. good _b_
2. rich ____
3. boring ____
4. happy ____
5. dangerous ____
6. difficult ____

a. easy
b. bad
c. safe
d. poor
e. unhappy
f. interesting

B Complete the sentences about jobs. Use your ideas.

1. Her job is dangerous. She's _a pilot_____.
2. His job is interesting. He's _____.
3. Her job is boring. She's _____.
4. His job is difficult. He's _____.
5. My job is _____. I'm _____.

C Complete the sentences with possessive adjectives (*my, your, his, her, their*).

1. Hello! _____ name is Yong-Min.
2. Ms. Costa is a photographer. _____ job is very interesting.
3. They're my brothers. _____ names are Martin and Julio.
4. You're a dancer! Is _____ job difficult?
5. I like my teacher. _____ name is Mr. Clark.
6. Mr. Shen likes _____ job. He's an engineer.

D Unscramble the questions. Then write your answers.

1. (your what name is) _____?
   _____.

2. (from you are where) _____?
   _____.

3. (you what do do) _____?
   _____.

4. (work is your interesting) _____?
   _____.

People 11

Lesson D READING AND WRITING

The World of Work

Today, many people go to work in new countries. Here, we'll learn about four people and their jobs.

Michael Murphy is a doctor. He's from Ireland, but he works in many countries. He says, "My work is sometimes dangerous, but it's always interesting. It's a difficult job, but I love helping people."

Natsuko Mori is from Osaka, Japan. She works in Brazil now. She says, "I'm a teacher in a language school. I teach Japanese to Brazilian students. My students are very good, and I like my job."

Shaukat Ali is a taxi driver in London, England. He's from Pakistan. He says, "I love my job! It's difficult because London is so big. But the people are very nice. I love talking to people from different countries, so it's an interesting job."

Moses Agba is a soccer player from Nigeria, in Africa. Now he plays for a team in Italy. He says, "People think my job is exciting. That's true, but it isn't easy. I like living in Italy, and I love playing soccer, so I'm a really happy person!"

A Read the sentences. Circle **T** for *true* or **F** for *false*.

1. Natsuko is Brazilian.   T   F
2. Shaukat works in a car.   T   F
3. Playing soccer is an easy job.   T   F
4. Michael's job is dangerous.   T   F
5. Shaukat's and Michael's jobs are boring.   T   F
6. Teaching Japanese is a difficult job.   T   F
7. Moses isn't happy.   T   F
8. These people like their jobs.   T   F

PEOPLE UNIT 1

B Write the person's name. You can repeat names.

1. _____ is Japanese.
2. _____ lives in Italy.
3. _____ works with students.
4. _____ has a dangerous job.
5. _____ works in a big city.
6. _____ is Irish.
7. _____ has an exciting job.
8. _____ loves talking to people.

C Look at the picture. Write sentences about Lina and her job. Use your own ideas.

Lina is Mexican, but she lives in France. She's _____

_____

_____

_____

_____

_____

_____

D Look at the picture. Write sentences about Dave and his job. Use your own ideas.

_____

_____

_____

_____

_____

_____

_____

_____

People 13

UNIT 1

Review

A Solve the crossword puzzle with vocabulary and grammar from this unit.

Across
4. not safe
6. not poor
7. He's from Canada. He's _____.
10. I'm from Mexico. I'm _____.
13. not easy
14. not interesting
16. They _____ students.

Down
1. She's from France. She's _____.
2. They're from Korea. They're _____.
3. I have a brother. _____ name is Hiroshi.
5. job
8. I _____ a journalist.
9. A _____ works in a school.
10. I like _____ job because it's exciting.
11. A _____ works in an airplane.
12. I'm _____ Colombia.
15. My name _____ Elisa.

B Write about you and your job or about somebody you know and his or her job. Use words from the unit.

_____
_____
_____
_____

14   Unit 1

WORK, REST, AND PLAY

UNIT 2

Lesson A GRAMMAR AND VOCABULARY

A Match the columns to make activities.

1. brush _j_
2. get ____
3. eat ____
4. go ____
5. take ____
6. catch ____
7. go to ____
8. take a ____
9. watch ____
10. visit ____
11. start ____
12. eat ____

a. work
b. the bus
c. breakfast
d. out
e. TV
f. up
g. nap
h. to bed
i. a shower
j. your teeth
k. friends
l. the movies

B What do you do every day? Write activities from exercise **A**.

get up, _____

_____

C Complete the sentences with prepositions of time (*in, on, at*).

1. Mark gets up _____ 4:00 _____ the morning. He's a policeman.
2. In my country, people take a shower _____ the evening.
3. I visit my friends _____ Sundays.
4. Katie works _____ Christmas. She's a nurse.
5. Our English class is _____ 2:30 _____ the afternoon.
6. Do you go to school _____ Saturdays?

D Look at the pictures and describe Elvin's weekday routine. Use the simple present tense.

_____
_____
_____
_____
_____

Lesson B GRAMMAR AND VOCABULARY

A Unscramble the questions. Then write answers that are true for you.

1. get up on time you do what Sundays ? _____
   _____

2. do in do the morning what you ? _____
   _____

3. you Sundays do eat out on ? _____
   _____

4. take a nap Sunday you on afternoon do ? _____
   _____

5. in the evening you go to the movies do ? _____
   _____

B Think about a person in your family. What does he or she do on Sunday? Complete the chart.

Name: _____

Sunday morning	He/She
Sunday afternoon	
Sunday evening	

C Write sentences about you and the person you wrote about in exercise **B**. Use *so*, *neither*, and *but*.

1. _I eat dinner out on Sundays and so does my sister._
2. _____
3. _____
4. _____

16 Unit 2

WORK, REST, AND PLAY   UNIT 2

Lesson C GRAMMAR AND VOCABULARY

> celebrate   fireworks   costume
> present   decorate   mask

A Label the pictures.

1. _____   2. _____

3. _____   4. _____   5. _____   6. _____

B Write the correct adverb of frequency above each line.

> usually   never   often
> sometimes   always

0 percent ←――――――――――――→ 100 percent

C Write the sentences again using the adverbs of frequency.

1. I visit my family on Thanksgiving. (usually)

   _____

2. American Independence Day is on July 4. (always)

   _____

3. We work on New Year's Day. (never)

   _____

4. It is cold in winter. (usually)

   _____

5. We give presents to our friends. (often)

   _____

D Write sentences about things you do on special celebrations in your country.

1. (never)   I never _____.
2. (always) _____.
3. (sometimes) _____.

Work, Rest, and Play   17

Lesson D READING AND WRITING

Happy New Year!

In the Netherlands, New Year's Day is always on January 1. It's very cold, so people stay home and clean their houses. They have a party with their friends, and they eat special food, like donuts. In the evening, they watch a funny TV program about the old year, and then there are fireworks.

In Iran, New Year's Day isn't in January. It's called Nowruz, and it's in March. People always buy new clothes and clean their houses. They make special food, like meat and rice. They visit all the people in their families and give them presents. It's a very busy time!

Chinese New Year is in January or February. The date is different every year. It's a big celebration that lasts for 15 days. People don't go to work. They clean their houses and send cards to their friends. They eat a big dinner with their families, and they give presents and money to all the children. At night, they watch fireworks.

WORK, REST, AND PLAY

UNIT 2

A Which country is it? Check (✓) the answers. You can have one, two, or three answers for each sentence.

New Year's Day celebrations	The Netherlands	Iran	China
1. People eat special food.			
2. People watch fireworks.			
3. It's in January.			
4. People give presents.			
5. It's a long celebration.			
6. People watch TV.			
7. People clean their houses.			

B Complete the sentences. Use your own ideas.

1. On New Year's Day, I _____
   _____
   _____ .

2. I would like to celebrate New Year's Day in (the Netherlands/Iran/China) because _____
   _____
   _____ .

C Write about your favorite celebration. What do people do?

_____
_____
_____
_____
_____
_____
_____
_____

Work, Rest, and Play 19

UNIT 2

Review

A Solve the crossword puzzle with vocabulary and grammar from this unit.

Across

3. She always _____ to bed at eleven o'clock.
6. He always _____ a shower at eight o'clock.
7. I _____ the bus at nine thirty.
9. We give _____ to our friends for Christmas.
11. I go to work _____ the morning.
12. In my _____ time, I play sports.
13. We usually _____ breakfast at home.
15. You cover your face with a _____.
16. I see my family _____ Sunday.

Down

1. She _____ her friends on Saturdays.
2. I never _____ TV.
4. I sometimes _____ a nap.
5. People _____ their houses with lights.
7. special clothing for a festival
8. a time to do special things
10. We sometimes eat _____ in restaurants.
12. We have _____ on special days.
14. I get up _____ seven o'clock.

B Describe your daily routine. Use words from the unit.

_____
_____
_____
_____

GOING PLACES

UNIT 3

Lesson A GRAMMAR AND VOCABULARY

claim   take   check   buy
pack   board go

A What are the steps in a trip? Write the correct verb in each sentence. You can use the verbs more than once.

1. You _____ your ticket from a travel agent.
2. You _____ your bags at home before your trip.
3. You _____ a taxi to the airport.
4. You _____ in when you get to the airport.
5. You take off your coat when you _____ through security.
6. Sometimes you _____ duty-free goods in a shop at the airport.
7. You can only take one small bag when you _____ the airplane.
8. You _____ your baggage at the baggage carousel.
9. Officers look at your passport when you _____ through immigration.
10. Customs officials look in your bag when you _____ through customs.

B Whose bag is this? Write three sentences about each picture.

1.
   a. It's my bag.
   b. It belongs to me.
   c. It's mine.

2.
   a. It's your _____
   b. _____
   c. _____

3.
   a. It's _____
   b. _____
   c. _____

4.
   a. _____
   b. _____
   c. _____

5.
   a. It's our bag.
   b. _____
   c. _____

6.
   a. _____
   b. _____
   c. _____

Going Places   21

Lesson B GRAMMAR AND VOCABULARY

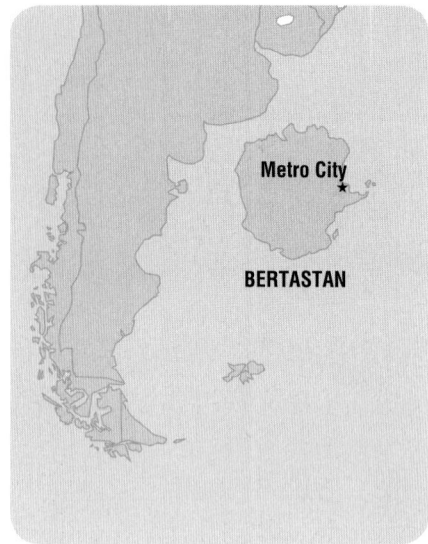

A Match the questions and answers.

1. Is this your first time in our country? ____
2. Where are you staying? ____
3. Is this your bag? ____
4. Can I see your passport, please? ____
5. Can I see your ticket, please? ____
6. What is the purpose of your visit? ____

a. Yes. Here it is.
b. I have an e-ticket. Here's the number.
c. No. I was here last year.
d. At the Grand Hotel.
e. I'm here on vacation.
f. No, it isn't. The brown bag is mine.

B Claudia Torres is traveling to Bertastan (a fictional island country) for her vacation. Complete the immigration form with her information.

> Argentinian   July 1, 1988   Claudia   Buenos Aires   Metro City   Torres
> Paradise Hotel, 118 Beach Road, Metro City   March 8th   business
> March 12th   Argentina

REPUBLIC OF BERTASTAN Immigration Form
1. Family name:
2. First name:
3. Date of birth:
4. Place of birth:
5. Nationality:
6. Country of residence:
7. Destination in this country:
8. Hotel address:
9. Entry date: Departure date:
10. Reason for visit:

C Mark the rising and falling tone in the sentences with ↗ ↘. Then say the sentences out loud.

1. Let's visit New ↗York, ↗Boston, and ↘Miami.

2. Here are my passport, visa, and ticket.

3. Every morning, I get up, take a shower, and read the newspaper.

4. We're going to China, Japan, Korea, and Thailand.

UNIT 3 GOING PLACES

Lesson C GRAMMAR AND VOCABULARY

A Write the correct word for each definition.

1. This has your name and photo in it: _passport_
2. You use these cards to buy things: _____
3. You need this to enter some countries: _____
4. You show this to get on an airplane: _____
5. You need this to drive a car in other countries: _____
6. You use this to buy things every day: _____
7. You need this if you get sick: _____

B Write advice about the answers in exercise **A** for travelers to your country.

1. You shouldn't bring a lot of cash. It isn't safe.
2. _____
3. _____
4. _____
5. _____

C Unscramble the questions. Write answers about your country using *should* or *shouldn't*.

1. rent I a car should _____?
   You _____ because _____.

2. I a warm coat should bring _____?
   You _____ because _____.

3. should insurance get travel I _____?
   You _____ because _____.

4. money I take should of lots _____?
   You _____ because _____.

5. take credit card a I should _____?
   You _____ because _____.

Going Places 23

Lesson D READING AND WRITING

Travel Light!

Even on a long trip, you don't need a lot of heavy suitcases. You need only two bags—a carry-on bag and a check-in bag. Here are some pointers for packing them.

Carry-on bag

- Your carry-on bag should be small and light.
- The most important things for your trip (passport, airline tickets, travel insurance documents, credit cards, cell phone, keys, etc.) should go in your carry-on bag.
- You should bring a change of clothes in case your luggage is delayed.
- You should also take medicine you need in your carry-on bag.
- Bring snacks to eat on the plane. Cookies, nuts, and dried fruit are good. Don't bring chocolate—it's very messy. For long trips, bring a sandwich. And don't bring water—you can't take it through security. You should buy some at the airport before you board the plane.
- Remember to bring a good book or your tablet.

Check-in bag

- Your check-in bag should be strong.
- Your clothes, shoes, and other everyday things should go in your check-in bag.
- Make a list to help you remember everything.
- Pack your bag early—don't pack on the same day as your trip!
- Think about the weather. Do you need a coat and gloves, or T-shirts and shorts? Choose the right clothes! You should pack your clothes inside plastic bags.
- Put your name and your hotel's address and telephone number on your bag. You should put this information inside the bag, too.

Have a great trip!

GOING PLACES — UNIT 3

A Answer true or false. Circle **T** for *true* or **F** for *false*.

1. You need three bags to go on a trip. — T F
2. Your carry-on bag should be big and strong. — T F
3. Your carry-on bag is for things you need on the airplane. — T F
4. Your check-in bag is for clothes and things you use on your vacation. — T F
5. You should put your home address on your check-in bag. — T F
6. You should pack your laptop in your check-in bag. — T F
7. You shouldn't take food in your carry-on bag. — T F
8. You should put your clothes in plastic bags. — T F

B Are these things good ideas or bad ideas?

	good idea	bad idea
1. packing your bags a few days before your trip		
2. putting your keys in your carry-on bag		
3. getting information about the weather before you pack		
4. packing chocolate in your check-in bag		
5. bringing water in your bags		
6. putting your name on your bags		
7. bringing a sandwich with you		
8. putting your credit card in your check-in bag		

C What do you pack in your bags for a trip? Why?

_____
_____
_____
_____
_____
_____
_____
_____
_____
_____

UNIT 3

Review

A Solve the crossword puzzle with vocabulary and grammar from this unit.

Across
2. It's their car. It belongs to _____.
3. I _____ my bags in the morning.
9. It's his book. It belongs to _____.
10. Show your passport at _____.
11. You _____ bring a sweater. It's a good idea.
12. It's your ticket. It's _____.
13. _____ house is it? It's Omar's.

Down
1. You need a _____ to go into this country.
2. I always _____ a taxi to the airport.
3. an ID with your name and photo
4. You buy things with a _____ card.
5. You go _____ security at the airport.
6. It's my bag. It's _____.
7. You need an international driver's _____ to rent a car.
8. You need travel _____ if you get sick.
14. It's our car. It's _____.

B Complete the travel advice with words from the box.

> pack   should   security
> credit card   board
> airline tickets   ~~should~~
> shouldn't   check in   your

Before you travel, you (1) __should__ check that you have (2) _____ travel documents: passport, visa, and (3) _____. You (4) _____ take a lot of cash with you. You (5) _____ take your (6) _____; it's safer. You should (7) _____ your bags the day before you travel, so you are ready. It's a good idea to get to the airport early because there are usually a lot of people. Remember: You need to (8) _____ first and then go through (9) _____ before you can (10) _____ the airplane. It can take a long time.

26   Unit 3

FOOD

Lesson A GRAMMAR AND VOCABULARY

A Write the names of the foods on the lines.

1. _____
2. _____
3. _____
4. _____
5. _____
6. _____
7. _____
8. _____
9. _____
10. _____
11. _____
12. _____
13. _____
14. _____
15. _____
16. _____

B Look at the picture in exercise **A**. What's in the kitchen? Complete the sentences with *a, an, some,* or *any*.

1. We have _____ cheese.
2. There isn't _____ soda.
3. Do we have _____ coffee?
4. We need _____ tomato for the salad.
5. There aren't _____ lemons.
6. We have _____ bananas.
7. Do you need _____ onion?
8. There is _____ juice.

C What's in your kitchen now? Write sentences about the food you have. Use *a, an, some,* and *any*.

1. _____
2. _____
3. _____
4. _____
5. _____
6. _____

Lesson B GRAMMAR AND VOCABULARY

A A waiter and a customer are in a restaurant. Unscramble the sentences in their conversation.

1. (are order ready you to)

   Waiter: _____?

2. (recommend what you would)

   Customer: _____?

3. (excellent the chicken is)

   Waiter: _____.

4. (come does chicken with salad the)

   Customer: _____?

5. (does yes it)

   Waiter: _____.

6. (a baked potato have I'll the and chicken)

   Customer: _____.

7. (like would else you anything)

   Waiter: _____?

8. (like I a glass of would mineral water)

   Customer: _____.

B Read the menu. Write a new conversation. Use your own ideas.

Waiter: _____

You: _____

Waiter: _____

You: _____

Waiter: _____

You: _____

Waiter: _____

You: _____

Main Dishes
Lemon Chicken
Half a chicken in lemon sauce, served with rice
Fried Fish
Three pieces of fish, served with fried potatoes
Grilled Steak
A large steak from the grill, served with salad and a baked potato

Side Dishes
Green salad
Tomato salad
Vegetable soup
Onion soup

Drinks
Cola
Mineral water
Coffee
Tea

UNIT 4 FOOD

Lesson C GRAMMAR AND VOCABULARY

A Label the foods.

1. _____ 2. _____ 3. _____ 4. _____

5. _____ 6. _____ 7. _____ 8. _____

B What should the people to the right eat? Write foods from Lesson **A** and Lesson **C** and your own ideas. Use *lots of*, *a few*, or *a little*.

C Write questions with *How much* or *How many* to ask about a person's weekly diet.

1. (salad) _How much salad do you eat?_
2. (apples) _____
3. (breakfast cereal) _____
4. (whole wheat bagels) _____
5. (popcorn) _____

lots of salad

D Answer the questions in exercise **C**. Write answers that are true for you. Use *lots of*, *a few*, or *a little*.

1. _I eat lots of salad._
2. _____
3. _____
4. _____
5. _____

lots of cheese

Food 29

Lesson D READING AND WRITING

International Recipes: Colcannon from Ireland

In Ireland, people use lots of potatoes in their cooking. Some traditional Irish recipes are *boxty* (potato pancakes), *champ* (mashed potato with onions), *shepherd's pie* (ground beef with carrots and peas with mashed potato on top), and *coddle* (mashed potato with meat and onion). Here we have a recipe for *colcannon*. It has lots of potatoes, and it's delicious! People in Ireland like to eat this dish in cold weather.

Ingredients:

- 500 grams (1 pound) of cabbage
- 4 large potatoes
- 2 onions
- ½ cup of milk
- salt
- pepper
- butter

Step 1 Cut the cabbage in large pieces. Put it in a pan with a little water and boil it for 10 minutes. Pour out the water.

Step 2 Cut the potatoes in pieces. Boil them in water for 15 minutes. The potatoes should be very soft. Pour out the water. Add salt and pepper and mash the potatoes.

Step 3 Cut 2 onions into small pieces. Cook them in ½ cup of milk for 10 minutes.

Step 4 In a large pan, mix the milk and onions with the potatoes. Then add the cabbage. Cook until it is hot.

Step 5 Put the hot colcannon in a large bowl. Add pieces of butter on top.

FOOD

UNIT 4

A Read the article and label the pictures on page 30.

B Write the numbers of the steps in the recipe below the pictures.

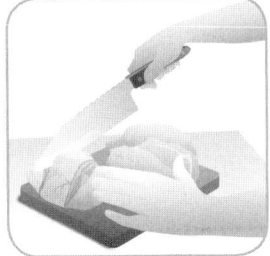  

_____ _____ _____

_____ _____

C Read the sentences. Circle **T** for *true* or **F** for *false*.

1. Colcannon is a cold food.　　　　　　　T　　F
2. Colcannon has three vegetables in it.　　T　　F
3. You cook the cabbage for colcannon.　　T　　F
4. You need some tomatoes for colcannon.　T　　F
5. You need some salt for colcannon.　　　T　　F

D Write about a famous food from your country. What are the ingredients? How do you make it? When do people eat it?

_____
_____
_____
_____
_____
_____

UNIT 4

Review

A Solve the crossword puzzle with vocabulary and grammar from this unit.

Across
1. How _____ money do you have?
4. We have a _____ milk.
6. bacon, steak, and sausages
7. We have _____ popcorn.
10. milk, cheese, and butter (2 words)
11. this person works in a restaurant
13. It's not important. It doesn't _____.
14. all the food you eat
15. I have _____ books. (2 words)
16. How _____ potatoes are there?

Down
2. a person who buys things
3. We have a _____ tomatoes.
5. tomatoes, onions, and potatoes
8. oranges, bananas, and apples
9. chicken, fish, and shrimp
10. water, tea, and juice
12. Do you have _____ fruit?
16. Never _____. It's not important.

B Describe your daily diet. Use words from the unit.

_____
_____
_____
_____

SPORTS

UNIT 5

Lesson A GRAMMAR AND VOCABULARY

A Unscramble the activities.

1. niikhg   h_____
2. bimcling   c_____
3. akgnit a krbea   t_____ a b_____
4. gsmiimwn   s_____
5. yiplang cesocr   p_____ s_____
6. gjgiogn   j_____
7. iflngti ghwtsei   l_____ w_____

B Write questions and answers about the pictures. Use the present continuous tense.

1.
   a. What are they doing now?
   b. They're cooking.

2.
   a. _____
   b. _____

3.
   a. _____
   b. _____

4.
   a. _____
   b. _____

5.
   a. _____
   b. _____

6.
   a. _____
   b. _____

C What are they doing now? Write sentences about friends and family members. Use your ideas and the present continuous tense.

1. My brother is playing computer games.
2. _____
3. _____
4. _____

Sports 33

Lesson B GRAMMAR AND VOCABULARY

A Label the pictures with phrases from the box.

> go to a ball game   study   go ice skating
> play basketball   go to a movie   fix the roof

1. _____

2. _____

3. _____

4. _____

5. _____

6. _____

B Today is a holiday. Look at these people's activities and write sentences with the simple present and present continuous tenses.

	Mondays	Today, Monday, May 1
Beth	clean her house	watch a movie
Eric	go to his office	sleep late
Ms. Tyson	teach classes	swim at the Sports Center
Yuki and Yoko	study English	take a break
Mr. Kim	drive a bus	watch a ball game

1. (Beth) _On Mondays, Beth usually cleans her house._
   Today, she is watching a movie.

2. (Eric) _On Mondays,_ _____
   Today, _____

3. (Ms. Tyson) _____
   _____

4. (Yuki and Yoko) _____
   _____

5. (Mr. Kim) _____
   _____

C Read the phone conversation. Write the verb in the simple present tense or the present continuous tense.

Jason: Hi, Rick. What are you doing?

Rick: Hi! You'll never guess. I (1) _____ (sit) in the living room at my parents' house.

Jason: Really? But you always (2) _____ (see) your cousin on Saturdays.

Rick: Not today. He (3) _____ (work), so I (4) _____ (visit) my parents. We (5) _____ (look) at vacation photos and (6) _____ (talk about) their trip. And my mother (7) _____ (cook) dinner!

34   Unit 5

SPORTS UNIT 5

Lesson C GRAMMAR AND VOCABULARY

A Write the sport for each item shown. In the boxes, write I (indoor) or O (outdoor) and T (team) or I (individual).

> ice hockey   gymnastics   baseball
> skateboarding   golf   football
> volleyball   diving

 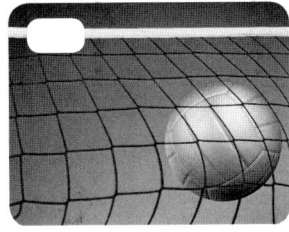  

1. _____   2. _____   3. _____   4. _____

5. _____   6. _____   7. _____   8. _____

B Read the phone conversation. Write the correct form of the verb—simple present tense or present continuous tense.

Andy: Hi, Yoshi. What (1) _are you doing_ (you, do)? It's very noisy there.

Yoshi: I (2) _____ (watch) a football game at the stadium! It's American football.

Andy: Really? (3) _____ (you, like) it?

Yoshi: Yes! But I (4) _____ (know, not) very much about the sport. Wow! Now all the players (5) _____ (run), and one player (6) _____ (throw) the ball.

Andy: And all the people (7) _____ (shout).

Yoshi: You should come to a game with me. The tickets only (8) _____ (cost) $5.

Andy: I (9) _____ (want, not) to watch football. I (10) _____ (hate) outdoor sports. I (11) _____ (prefer) to be inside.

Yoshi: What (12) _____ (you, do) today?

C Answer the questions. Write complete sentences.

1. What sport do you like? Why? _____

2. What sport do you hate? Why? _____

Lesson D READING AND WRITING

Sports Around the World

Soccer is very popular in Brazil. It's a great sport for people of all ages. You don't need much—just a ball and a place to play. You can play on a team, or you can just play with your friends. Soccer is popular in every country around the world. It's really an international sport.

In Canada, people love ice hockey. It's very cold in winter, but people don't like to stay indoors. Children play ice hockey at school. People watch their games and drink hot chocolate! Of course, people also watch famous hockey teams on TV.

One of the most popular sports in the United States is baseball. Some people think it's very slow, but it's a really interesting game. It's fun to sit outdoors with your friends at a baseball game. People eat hot dogs and cheer for their team.

A lot of people in China play volleyball. There are teams at schools and offices. You can play volleyball indoors or outdoors. It's a good sport because you don't need expensive equipment. The only things you need are a ball and a net.

SPORTS
UNIT 5

A Read the article and complete the chart.

Country	Sport	Good things about the sport
Brazil		great for people _____ you need _____ and _____ it's _____ sport
	ice hockey	children play _____ people _____ at the games also watch _____
United States		it's _____, but it's _____ sit outdoors with _____ people eat _____ at the game
		teams at _____ and _____ can play _____ or _____ don't need _____

B Write about a popular sport in your country. Who plays it? Who watches it? What equipment do you need? Where do you play it? Do you like it? Why or why not?

_____

_____

_____

_____

_____

_____

_____

_____

UNIT 5

Review

A Solve the crossword puzzle with vocabulary and grammar from this unit.

Across
2. I'm tired, so I'm taking a _____.
3. On Saturdays I _____ ice skating.
5. We (cook) _____ dinner every day.
6. "I like basketball." "Me, _____."
7. You do this sport in a pool.
9. "I don't like tennis." "Me, _____."
13. not outdoor
15. Rock _____ is a dangerous sport.
16. I (study) _____ right now. (2 words)
17. I (know) _____ a lot about sports.

Down
1. I lift _____ at the gym.
4. Baseball is a _____ sport. People do it together.
5. It's expensive. It _____ a lot of money.
8. Diving is an _____ sport. There are no teams.
10. things you need for a sport
11. He (prefer) _____ outdoor sports.
12. running
14. I like to _____ soccer.

B Write about what you usually do on the weekend and what you are doing now. Use words from the unit.

_____
_____
_____

DESTINATIONS

UNIT 6

Lesson A GRAMMAR AND VOCABULARY

rent   take a   check in
take   visit   unpack   buy

A Complete the expressions for vacation activities.

1. _____ places of interest
2. _____ bus tour
3. _____ to the hotel
4. _____ a car
5. _____ photos
6. _____ your suitcases
7. _____ souvenirs

B Write the past tense form of the verb. Be careful! Some verbs have -ed endings, and some verbs are irregular.

1. see	saw	9. buy	
2. help		10. travel	
3. take		11. know	
4. ask		12. leave	
5. need		13. play	
6. fly		14. tell	
7. say		15. eat	
8. go		16. learn	

C Look at the pictures and complete the conversation. Use the words in parentheses to write questions and answers in the simple past tense.

Eric: Tell me about your vacation! (1) _Where did you go_ (where/go)?

Katie: (2) _____ (we/go/to India). It was great!

Eric: (3) _____ (where/fly to)?

Katie: (4) _____ (fly/to New Delhi). We stayed for two nights. (5) _____ (then/take/a train to Agra).

Eric: (6) _____ (what/do in Agra)?

Katie: (7) _____ (we/visit/the Taj Mahal). It was beautiful!

Eric: What about the food in India? (8) _____ (you/like it)?

Katie: Yes! (9) _____ (we/go/to some great restaurants).

Destinations 39

Lesson B GRAMMAR AND VOCABULARY

A Read about the tour. Imagine you took the tour. Write sentences in the simple past tense.

A Week in Paris! Only $1,995!

Monday	Leave home and fly to Paris. Go to the hotel.
Tuesday	Visit the Eiffel Tower.
Wednesday	See all the famous paintings in the Louvre Museum.
Thursday	Take a boat trip on the Seine River.
Friday	Watch artists in Montmartre, and have dinner in a French restaurant.
Saturday	Go shopping at a famous department store and buy souvenirs.
Sunday	Go to the airport. Then return home.

1. _On Monday, I left home and flew to Paris. I_____.
2. _On Tuesday, I_____.
3. _____
4. _____
5. _____
6. _____
7. _____

B Two people are talking about a vacation. Write the questions.

1. **Q:** _____?
   A: I went to Buenos Aires, in Argentina.

2. **Q:** _____?
   A: I stayed there for a week.

3. **Q:** _____?
   A: I visited all the famous places and ate great steaks.

4. **Q:** _____?
   A: I bought a cool jacket.

5. **Q:** _____?
   A: Yes, I really enjoyed it! It's a beautiful city!

DESTINATIONS   UNIT 6

Lesson C GRAMMAR AND VOCABULARY

A Complete the sentences with the emphatic adjectives from the box. Use each word once.

> horrible   huge   filthy   fascinating   ~~excellent~~   spotless   exhausting

1. The museum was good. In fact, I think it was _____excellent_____.
2. The books were interesting. In fact, I think they were _____.
3. The food in the restaurant was bad. In fact, I think it was _____.
4. My hotel room was very clean. In fact, I think it was _____.
5. The trip was really tiring. In fact, I think it was _____.
6. The beaches were very dirty. In fact, I think they were _____.
7. The store was very big. In fact, I think it was _____.

B Complete the sentences with your own ideas.

1. _____ is outstanding.
2. _____ are amazing.
3. _____ is awful.
4. _____ is magnificent.
5. _____ are terrible.
6. _____ is enormous.

C Complete the sentences with *was*, *wasn't*, *were*, and *weren't*.

1. Jacob ____wasn't____ in class yesterday because he ____was____ sick.
2. The stores _____ open last Monday because it _____ a holiday.
3. I didn't like my vacation. The hotel _____ horrible, and the restaurants _____ expensive.
4. I got 90 percent on that test. It _____ very long, and the questions _____ easy.
5. Where _____ you last night? I called you, but you _____ home.

D Complete the conversations.

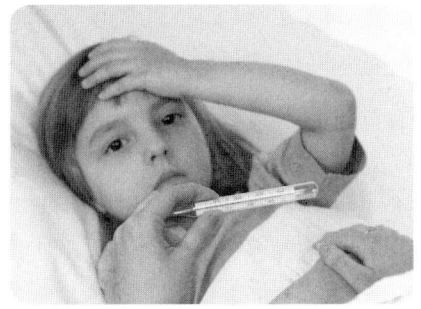  

1. **A:** _____ Alina at school yesterday?
   B: No, she _____. She _____ at home.

2. **A:** _____ you in Mexico on vacation?
   B: No, _____. _____ in Brazil.

3. **A:** _____ Rick at the Sports Center on Saturday?
   B: No, _____. _____ at the library.

Destinations 41

Lesson D READING AND WRITING

Andy's vacation

To: jj@gomail.com
From: andy2000@hitmail.com
Subject: Good and Bad

Hi Jessica,

You asked about my vacation. There was good and bad.

It was a long trip. The airline was terrible. Everything was late, and the airplane was filthy, with food on the floor and papers everywhere. We flew to the capital city, and then we took a train. We took a boat to get to White Beach. We left home at 5:00 a.m., and we arrived at 10:00 p.m.

The beach was amazing! It really is white, and it's very clean. In fact, it was spotless, and the water was warm and blue. We went swimming every day and walked on the beach. Our hotel was huge but very nice. The food was OK, but the restaurants had only a few different dishes. We had fish every day.

One day, we took a bus tour. It was exhausting! We went to about 20 different places. We only stayed for 10 minutes at each place, so we didn't have time to take photos. And the tour guide was terrible. He didn't speak English very well.

At the end of our vacation, we went to a gift shop. They had some nice souvenirs there. I bought T-shirts for all my friends. I have a T-shirt for you, too!

See you soon!

Andy

DESTINATIONS — UNIT 6

A Circle the correct answer.

1. Andy stayed at ___.
   a. the capital city b. a beach c. a small town
2. His trip to White Beach was ___.
   a. easy b. hard c. short
3. The hotel was ___.
   a. big b. dirty c. fascinating
4. The food wasn't ___.
   a. healthy b. interesting c. delicious

B What did Andy think about these things? Check (✓) his opinions.

	☺	😐	☹
1. his vacation			
2. the airplane			
3. the beach			
4. the hotel			
5. the food			
6. the bus tour			
7. the souvenirs			

C You took a vacation in London. Look at the vacation information. Write an e-mail to your friend about it.

Your London Tour

- fly to Heathrow Airport
- five days in a big hotel
- eat in English restaurants
- visit the Tower of London
- see Buckingham Palace
- take a boat trip on the Thames River
- buy souvenirs in famous department stores

___
___
___
___
___
___
___

UNIT 6

Review

A Solve the crossword puzzle with vocabulary and grammar from this unit.

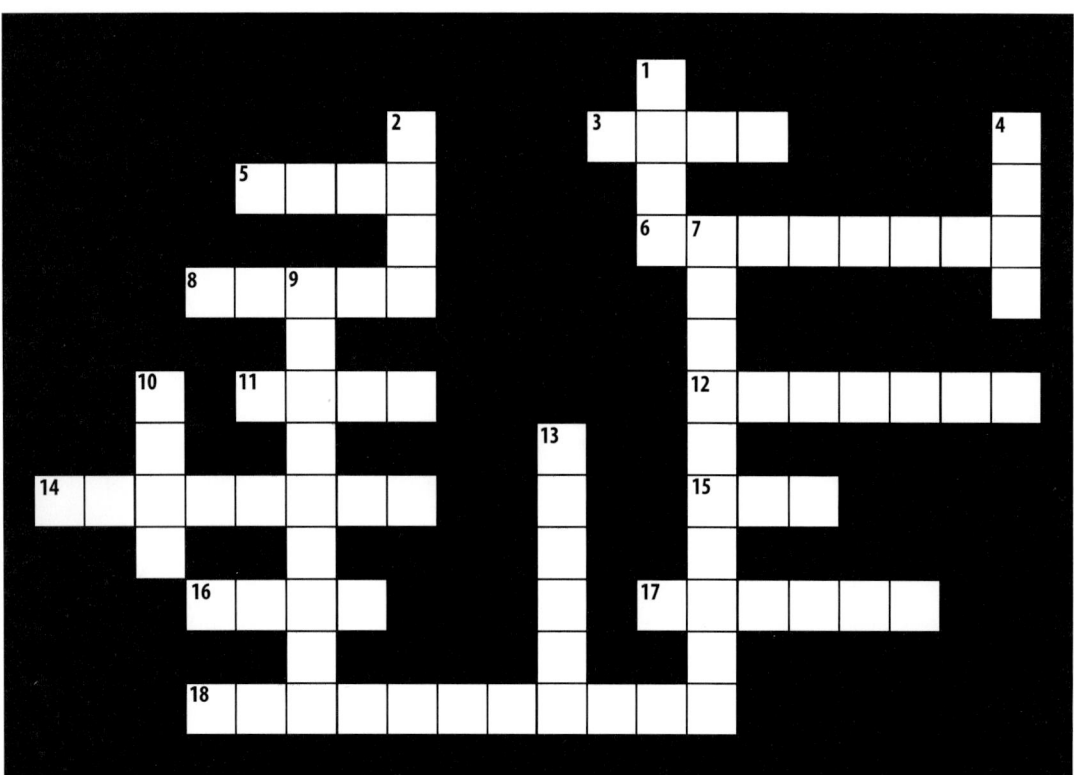

Across
3. past tense of *go*
5. I like to _____ photos.
6. very bad
8. I always _____ places of interest on vacation.
11. very big
12. very good
14. very clean
15. past tense of *see*
16. past tense of *say*
17. very dirty
18. very interesting

Down
1. past tense of *leave*
2. I always _____ a car to drive on vacation.
4. past tense of *fly*
7. very tiring
9. I always buy _____ to remember my vacation.
10. past tense of *take*
13. past tense of *buy*

B Describe a vacation you took. Use words from the unit.

_____
_____
_____
_____